Contents

Encourage Your Child to Develop a Growth Mindset

The research of psychologist Dr. Carol Dweck tells us that people have two possible mindsets—a fixed mindset or a growth mindset. People with a fixed mindset believe that they are either smart or good at something, or they are not—and nothing can change that. People with a growth mindset believe that it is always possible to get better at doing something. Dr. Dweck has found that students with a growth mindset are more motivated to learn and achieve more than students with a fixed mindset.

How can you help your child develop a growth mindset?

Talk about the brain. Explain that the brain becomes stronger by working hard to master new skills. Just as exercise makes muscles stronger, working at challenging thinking tasks makes the brain stronger.

View mistakes as learning opportunities. Let your child know that mistakes are valuable ways of learning where the problems lie. By carefully looking at mistakes, you and your child can learn where there are misunderstandings or missing pieces of knowledge. Mistakes pave the way to success!

Teach ways of dealing with frustration. Children can "turn off" when they become frustrated, which makes learning impossible. Teach your child ways to overcome frustration. For example, use the Internet to learn about breathing techniques that combat stress. You can also remind your child of skills that he or she mastered in the past (such as learning to tie shoelaces) that took time and effort to learn.

Focus on praising the process. While it's fine to praise your child or the results he or she achieved, you can encourage a growth mindset by focusing your praise on the process. For example, praise your child's willingness to keep trying and his or her use of effective learning strategies, such as asking questions.

Model a growth mindset. Look for opportunities to reinforce with your child how to see things from a growth mindset. For example:

If your child says...	Respond by saying...
I'll never get this!	Maybe you can't do it yet, but you'll get better if you keep trying.
I've been working at this for a long time and I'm still not getting it right.	Look at these areas where you've made progress. Keep working and you'll make more progress.
Hey, I can finally do this!	Let's think about how you achieved success. Some of the things you did this time might help you with the next challenge.

MONDAY • Sentences and Punctuation

A *sentence* is group of words that express a complete thought.
A *sentence fragment* is a group of words that don't form a complete sentence.

1. Circle the complete sentence. Underline the sentence fragment.

   a) Seashells on the beach.   b) I collected seashells on the beach.

2. The *complete subject* contains all the words that tell who or what the sentence is about. Circle the complete subject.

   a) The soccer game is on Sunday afternoon.

   b) The neighbourhood children played baseball in the field.

3. The *complete predicate* includes the verb and all the words that tell about what happened in the sentence. Underline the complete predicate.

   a) The soccer game is on Sunday afternoon.

   b) The neighbourhood children played baseball in the field.

TUESDAY • Grammar and Usage

Common nouns name people, places, and things that are not specific.
Verbs are action words. *Adjectives* are describing words.

1. Sort the words into the correct category.

   tree drive sky song happy feel paper wonderful kind sit house beach
   clear mall sing play watch large run baseball fast mountain tiny dance

   Nouns: tree, sky, paper, house, beach, mall, baseball

   Verbs: drive, sit, sing, play, run, dance mountain

   Adjectives: large, song, happy, feel, wonderful, kind, clear, watch, fast, tiny

2. *Proper nouns* are words that name specific people or pets, places, holidays, days of the week, and months of the year. Proper nouns begin with a capital letter.

   Examples: Cindy   Masonville Mall   Valentine's Day   September   Monday

   Write two examples of a proper noun. Haloween, Ryan

   spelling

WEDNESDAY • Figures of Speech

1. *Alliteration* is when two or more words in a phrase or sentence start with the same sound.

   Examples: Shelley showed Simon seven slimy slugs.
   Carla was calm, cool, and collected.

   Underline the letters or sounds that repeat.

   a) Leila loves the little lake which is lined with lovely lilies.

   b) Casey cut the cloth to create a cute carryall.

2. An *analogy* compares two things that seem different, and shows the relationship between them.

   Examples: night = dark as day = light   apple = fruit as carrot = vegetable

   Write the missing word.

   a) fork = eat as cup = _____   **b)** kitten = cat as puppy = _____

THURSDAY • Vocabulary and Spelling

1. **A *root* or *base word* is a word that has a prefix or suffix added to it.**

Base word	With prefix *re*	With suffix *ing*
build	rebuild	building

   Identify and write the base word.

   a) readable _____   **b)** unimportant _____

2. **A *synonym* is a word that has the same meaning as another word. Circle the synonym for the bolded word.**

   a) close sweater   shut   **b) joy** anger   happiness

3. **An *antonym* is a word that has the opposite meaning to another. Circle the antonym for the bolded word.**

   a) all   everything   none   **b) best**   worst   finest

FRIDAY • Writing Prompt

A *proverb* is a saying that offers some advice on how to live your life.

1. a) **Explain what you think the proverb below means. Draw the saying.**

"Every cloud has a silver lining."

_____

_____

b) **Do you think this is good advice? Explain your thinking.**

_____

_____

_____

_____

☐ I checked for correct spelling.
☐ I checked for correct punctuation.
☐ I used interesting words.

☐ I organized my ideas in a way that makes sense.
☐ I used linking words to connect my ideas.
☐ Challenge: I used a figure of speech.

MONDAY • Sentences and Punctuation

A *statement* is a sentence that ends with a *period*. (.)

A *question* is a sentence that ends with a *question mark*. (?)

An *exclamation* is a sentence that shows strong feeling, such as excitement, joy, or anger. It ends with an *exclamation mark*. (!)

A *command* is a sentence that tells someone to do something. It can end with a *period* (.) or with an *exclamation mark*. (!)

1. Write the correct punctuation mark at the end of each sentence.

a) This is my favourite __!__   b) Would you like some water __?__

c) Eat your vegetables __!__   d) Tomorrow is Tuesday __.__

2. Read the sentence. Circle the complete subject. Underline the complete predicate.

Andrew and Pria went to the soccer championship game.

TUESDAY • Grammar and Usage

1. The words *a* and *an* are called *articles*.
Use *a* before a specific singular noun that starts with a consonant.
Use *an* before a specific singular noun that starts with a vowel.

a) _____ panda   b) _____ egg   c) _____ ostrich   d) _____ chair

2. Underline the common nouns and circle the proper nouns.

On Sunday, Mr. Turnbull went to Milton Park for a hike and to watch birds.

3. Circle the adjective in each sentence. Underline the noun it describes.

a) A black spider crawled up the wall.   b) This is my favourite toy.

4. Underline the verb in each sentence.

a) A pack of wolves howled at the bright moon.

b) The police arrested a thief outside the jewellery store.

WEDNESDAY • Figures of Speech

Hyperboles are extreme exaggerations used for emphasis and humour.

Examples: Ted is so angry, he might explode!   I am so hungry I could eat a horse.

1. Finish the sentence using hyperbole.

She is moving slower than a _____ !

2. A *metaphor* is a kind of comparison of two things. It does not use the words *like* or *as*; instead, a metaphor suggests something actually *is* something else.

Example: Jerome is a <u>night owl</u>.

The phrase "night owl" means Jerome likes to stay up late.

In this metaphor, circle the correct meaning of the underlined phrase.

My dog, Frankie, <u>is a chicken</u>.

(is actually a chicken instead of a dog   is scared of everything)

THURSDAY • Vocabulary and Spelling

A *homophone* is a word which sounds like another word, but which has a different spelling and meaning.

Examples: to, two, too   pear, pair   there, their, they're

1. Fill in the blank with the correct word.

a) _____ is my favourite colour.   (Blew   Blue)

b) The wind _____ my hat off my head.   (blew   blue)

2. Circle the synonym for the bolded word.

a) **city** office   town   b) **during** while   after   c) **glue** shift   stick

3. Circle the definition of the word *dress*.   (put on clothes   wipe something clean)

FRIDAY • Writing Prompt

A *recount* tells about events in the order that they happened.
Write a recount of a visit you made to a special place. Draw the event.

_____

_____

_____

_____

_____

_____

☐ I told the order of events with words like first, next, then, before, after, and finally.

☐ I ordered my ideas in a way that makes sense.

☐ I used "I" or "we" in my writing.

☐ I made sure to include details that answer who, what, where, when, and why.

☐ I checked for correct spelling and punctuation.

MONDAY • Sentences and Punctuation

1. A *conjunction* is a word that joins two sentences or ideas. Fill in the blank with the correct conjunction.

Does the clover have three leaves, _____ does it have four leaves?   (so or)

2. Rewrite the sentence using correct capitalization and punctuation.

the city of ottawa is the capital of Canada

_____

3. a) What is missing in the sentence fragment below? Circle the answer.

the new boy in our class

(who or what is doing the action   the action   both are missing)

b) Rewrite the sentence fragment. Add what is missing to make a complete sentence.

_____

TUESDAY • Grammar and Usage

1. Make the nouns plural by adding *s*. Add *es* to nouns that end with *s, x, ch,* or *sh*. For nouns that end with a consonant + *y*, change the *y* to an *i* and add *es*.

a) box _____   b) glass _____   c) doll _____   d) fly _____

e) book _____   f) wish _____   g) beach _____   h) fox _____

2. Circle the word in brackets that best completes the sentence.

a) I wonder if Mario (can must) speak Spanish.

b) Tamara isn't sure, but she (will might) go to the movie with us.

3. Circle all the adjectives in the sentence. Underline the noun each adjective describes. Draw an arrow from each adjective to the noun it describes.

Use cold water to rinse the fresh vegetables.

WEDNESDAY • Figures of Speech

Similes are phrases that use the words *as* or *like* to describe something or someone.

Examples: That old dog is as blind as a bat.   That quiz was as easy as ABC!

1. Put a check mark beside the sentence that contains a simile.

a) As I walked to the library, I saw Todd. _____

b) My new baby sister is as cute as a button. _____

2. Finish the sentence using hyperbole.

Nazeem was so happy, his smile was a _____ wide!

3. Complete the analogy.

thirsty = drink   as   hungry = _____

THURSDAY • Vocabulary and Spelling

1. Circle the antonym for the bolded word.

a) accept   take   refuse   b) attic   rooftop   basement

2. Circle the synonyms for the word *energy*.

power   mean   helpful   force   gentle   strength   mood

3. Complete each sentence with the correct word.

a) The recipe calls for two cups of _____ . (flour   flower)

b) My grandmother's favourite _____ is a rose. (flour   flower)

4. An *abbreviation* is the short form of a word. It ends with a period. Write the abbreviation for each word.

a) Saturday _____   b) Tuesday _____   c) Friday _____

FRIDAY • Writing Prompt

A *procedure* is a set of numbered steps to follow to make or do something. Write a procedure for something that is easy to make or do.

Description

_____

Materials or Ingredients

_____

_____

_____

Instructions

_____

_____

_____

_____

_____

_____

_____

_____

_____

☐ I have a description that tells what you will make or do.

☐ The information is organized under headings.

☐ I used sequencing words such as first, then, next and finally.

☐ I used action words to tell which actions to do.

☐ I checked for correct spelling and punctuation.

MONDAY • Sentences and Punctuation

1. A *run-on sentence* joins two or more sentences that should be written separately.
   For each sentence below, write *RO* if it is a run-on sentence.
   Put a check mark if the sentence is correct.

   a) Holden threw the ball it went over the wall. _____

   b) I need gloves since it is cold outside. _____

2. Add the correct punctuation mark to the end of each sentence.
   Name the sentence type.

   a) Would you like some celery sticks _____   _____

   b) Put the plates, cutlery, and glasses on the table _____   _____

3. Use a comma between the day and the year in a date.

   My brother's birthday is June 15 2002.

TUESDAY • Grammar and Usage

1. *A pronoun* is a word that takes the place of one or more nouns.
   Choose the correct pronoun to take the place of nouns that name people.

   I   you   he   she   we   they   him   her   them   us

   a) Zac and Katie _____   b) Sara _____   c) Logan and I _____

2. A *preposition* is a word that tells *where* a person, animal, place, or thing is.
   Some examples are *in, on, under, behind,* and *over.*
   Circle the preposition in the sentence.

   My socks are under the bed.

3. Complete the sentence by writing the past tense of the verb in brackets.

   a) This word once _____ (mean) something different than it does now.

   b) Last night, I _____ (lie) on the ground and looked up at the stars.

WEDNESDAY • Figures of Speech

1. Underline the letters that repeat the same sound.

a) Billy the bulldog bounces the brown ball.

b) Ellie the elephant eats everything.

2. Circle the correct meaning of the underlined phrase.

Ani is <u>feeling blue</u> today.

(feels like wearing something blue   feels sad)

3. Complete the similes.

a) Paul got wet in the rain. He looked like _____ .

b) Her pillow was as soft as _____ .

THURSDAY • Vocabulary and Spelling

A *contraction* is one word made from two words, with one or more of the letters left out. The letters that are left out are replaced with an *apostrophe* (').

1. Write the contraction for each pair of words.

a) I have _____ (I've   I'll)   **b)** you have _____ (you've   you'll)

2. Complete the sentence by writing *to* or *too*.

The soup is _____ hot _____ eat.

3. Circle the word that *does not* belong in the group.

rain   snow   hail   sun   ice

4. Read the sentence. Underline the word that has a suffix.

Our new neighbour next door is very friendly.

FRIDAY • Writing Prompt

Persuasive writing gives your opinion and tries to convince the reader to agree with you.

Read the statement below. Write a persuasive paragraph to convince the reader of your opinion. Make sure to add details to support your thinking.

"Breakfast is the most important meal of the day."

I (agree, <u>disagree</u>) that breakfast is the most important meal of the day.

First of all, I don't usually eat Breakfist in the morning.

Because I aready have enough energy

Another reason I don't lik fill my somch firstThing in the merning.

Also, Brecetit is not the most inPortit meal of the day.

This is why I think Braefus not the best meal.

☑ I clearly stated my opinion.

☑ I stated strong reasons and gave details.

☑ I organized my ideas in a way that makes sense.

☐ I used linking words to connect my ideas.

☐ I checked for correct spelling and punctuation.

MONDAY • Sentences and Punctuation

Use commas to separate three or more items in a series.
Put a comma after each item in the series, except for the last one.

Example: I like apples, pears, and bananas.

1. Add commas to separate the items in a series in the sentences below.

   a) My favourite colours are blue red and purple.

   b) For lunch we had sandwiches carrot sticks and chocolate milk.

   c) Robins cardinals and blue jays are types of birds.

2. Fill in the blank with the best conjunction.

   a) My aunt has two apple trees, _____ she has a pear tree.   (and   but)

   b) My cousin is older than me, _____ I am taller.   (and   but)

TUESDAY • Grammar and Usage

1. An *adverb* describes a verb. An adverb can describe *when* an action happens. Underline the adverb that tells when an action happens. Circle the verb.

   a) Come visit today.   **b)** Later, my friend and I are going for a hike.

   c) Tonight we have a baseball game.   **d)** I am going shopping tomorrow.

2. Circle the word in brackets that best completes the sentence.

   a) You (can   must) be tired after walking for four hours.

   b) They (will   might) wear space suits when outside the space station.

3. Circle the correct verb.

   a) Milk or juice (is   are) healthier for you than pop.

   b) Two escalators and an elevator (take   takes) people to the second floor.

WEDNESDAY • Figures of Speech

1. Is this an example of alliteration? Circle YES or NO.

a) Sami took his books back to the library.   **YES   NO**

b) Nimble Ned never needs new knights.   **YES   NO**

2. Complete the analogy by adding the missing word.

cold = ice   as   hot = _____

3. Put a check mark beside the hyperbole.

a) The book I ordered will never get here! _____   **b)** That's a really big turtle! _____

4. Complete the simile.

Molly is as happy as a _____ .

THURSDAY • Vocabulary and Spelling

1. Choose the best word to complete the sentence.

Peach and vanilla are good, but I think strawberry is the _____ . (best   better)

2. Circle the words that have a silent *e*.

sleep   cake   shed   are

3. Circle the synonyms for the word *bring*.

fetch   buy   get   simple   obtain   mess   retrieve   take

4. Identify and write the base word.

a) unimpressed _____

b) speechless _____

FRIDAY • Writing Prompt

In an *acrostic* poem, the first letter of each line forms a word or phrase (vertically). An acrostic poem can describe the subject or even tell a brief story about it.

Write an acrostic poem to describe yourself using the letters of your name.

_____ _____

_____ _____

_____ _____

_____ _____

_____ _____

_____ _____

_____ _____

_____ _____

_____ _____

_____ _____

_____ _____

_____ _____

☐ I used interesting words.   ☐ I checked for correct spelling and punctuation.

MONDAY • Sentences and Punctuation

Use *quotation marks* (" ") around words that someone is speaking. A speaker tag tells who is speaking. When the speaker tag comes after the spoken words, remember to put a comma before the second, or closing, quotation mark.

Examples: *"Please hand in your papers," the teacher said.*

"I have a secret," whispered Sally.

1. Add quotation marks and commas as necessary to each sentence.

   a) I hope we have good weather on the weekend Dad said.

   b) I wonder if she noticed that we came in late whispered Nicole.

2. Change the statement to a question.

The train is on time.

_____

TUESDAY • Grammar and Usage

Add an apostrophe and *s* to a singular noun to show possession.

Examples: the <u>tree's</u> branches, the <u>mouse's</u> tail, the <u>car's</u> tires

Add just an apostrophe to a plural noun that ends with *s*.

Examples: the babies' blankets, the students' notebooks

Add an apostrophe and *s* to a plural noun that does *not* end with *s*.

Examples: the people's coats, the men's laughter

1. Add an apostrophe or an apostrophe and *s* to form possessive nouns.

   a) the animals_____ habitat   **b)** the shark_____ teeth

   c) the five geese _____ feathers   **d)** the spider_____ web

WEDNESDAY • Figures of Speech

1. Choose a letter or sound and write a sentence using alliteration. Read it to a partner.

_____

2. Complete the analogy by adding the missing word.

hard = soft   as   tall = _____

3. Put a check mark beside the hyperbole.

My little brother never stops talking! ____   My ankle really hurts! ____

4. In this hyperbole, circle the correct meaning of the underlined phrase.

Our new house cost a <u>zillion dollars</u>!

(actually cost a zillion dollars   cost a lot of money)

THURSDAY • Vocabulary and Spelling

1. Identify and write the base word.

a) disappear _____   b) correction _____

2. Circle the synonym for _error_.

happening   mistake   painful

3. Circle the antonym for the bolded word.

a) **find**   lose   serious   b) **often**   never   quickly

4. Write the compound word.

a) after + noon = _____   b) no + thing = _____

5. Words can sometimes have a positive or a negative connotation, or meaning. Underline the phrase that has a negative connotation.

a) touch something   pinch something   b) pull hair   fluff hair

FRIDAY • Writing Prompt

Would you rather work on the computer or play outside? Explain your thinking.

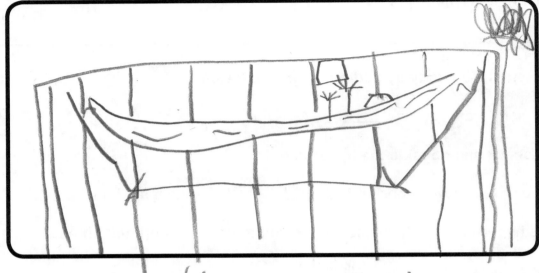

I would rather play out side on my
Phone in a hammok. beoucse I
would not what to spend 2 hour
working. It would be warm
and sunny. Also, a hammock is
holaxing.

- ☑ I checked for correct spelling.
- ☑ I checked for correct punctuation.
- ☑ I used interesting words.
- ☑ I organized my ideas in a way that makes sense.
- ☑ I used linking words to connect my ideas.
- ☑ Challenge: I used a figure of speech.

MONDAY • Sentences and Punctuation

1. Add commas to separate the items in a series.

I have a pet fish, hamster, and cat.

2. Use quotation marks around words that someone is speaking. Add quotation marks and commas as necessary.

"I think the test is on Thursday," Julie said.

3. Rewrite the sentence using correct capitalization and punctuation.

mr. and mrs sully are going to mario's pizzeria for dinner

_____

4. Correct the run-on sentence by writing it as two sentences.

Spot is chasing a cat Spot won't stop.

_____

TUESDAY • Grammar and Usage

1. Change the *f* to a *v* and add *es* to make these nouns plural.

a) loaf _____   b) wolf _____   c) scarf _____

2. Add the letter *s* to these nouns that end with *f* to make them plural.

a) chef _____   b) cliff _____   c) roof _____

3. Underline the verb in the sentence.

The artist sketches portraits of people on the street.

4. Write the correct pronoun to complete each sentence.

a) Felix and _____ have known each other for two years.   (I   me)

b) Mom gave my brother and _____ some crafts to do.   (I   me)

shannon

shannon

WEDNESDAY • Figures of Speech

1. *Onomatopoeia* **is the use of a word that sounds like what it names.**

Examples: crash   buzz   ding dong   meow

Read each sentence below. Underline the words or words that are examples of onomatopoeia.

a) Listen to the pig say "oink, oink" as it munches its food.

b) I heard the cow moo at the farmer.   **c)** The dog barked at the cat.

2. An *oxymoron* **is a pair of words that have opposite meanings placed side by side for effect.**

Examples: pretty ugly   big baby

Fill in the blanks using the examples of oxymoron above.

That sweater is _____ .   You are acting like a _____ !

THURSDAY • Vocabulary and Spelling

1. Write the *prefix*, the *suffix*, and the *base word*.

Word	Prefix	Suffix	Base word
unfolding			
discounted			

2. How many syllables are there in the word *chocolate*? _____

3. A word that rhymes with *mail* is _____

4. Underline the positive words. Circle the negative words.

nonsense   fluffy   sparkling   itchy   cheerful   grouchy   sore

FRIDAY • Writing Prompt

A *proverb* is a saying that offers some advice on how to live your life.

1. a) Explain what you think the proverb below means. Draw the proverb.

"Without wood, a fire goes out."

_____

_____

b) Do you think this is good advice? Explain your thinking.

_____

_____

_____

_____

☐ I checked for correct spelling.   ☐ I organized my ideas in a way that makes sense.

☐ I checked for correct punctuation.   ☐ I used linking words to connect my ideas.

☐ I used interesting words.   ☐ Challenge: I used a figure of speech.

MONDAY • Sentences and Punctuation

Use quotation marks around words that someone is speaking. When the speaker tag comes after the spoken words, do not put a comma before the second quotation mark if there is a question mark or exclamation point at the end of the spoken words.

Examples: *"Who left the door open?" asked Ray.*

            "That is so amazing!" exclaimed Shauna.

1. Add quotation marks to each sentence.

   a) Would you like to look through the telescope? the scientist asked.

   b) We won the championship! shouted Mike.

2. Read the sentence. Circle the complete subject. Underline the complete predicate.

   The tall tree swayed dangerously in the strong wind.

TUESDAY • Grammar and Usage

1. Circle the word in brackets that best completes the sentence.

   a) The law says that drivers (might   must) come to a stop at a stop sign.

   b) Some high speed trains (can   will) go much faster than a regular train.

2. Complete the sentence by writing the past tense of the verb in brackets.

   a) The police _____ (catch) the burglar climbing out of a window.

   b) The buildings _____ (shake) during the earthquake.

3. Underline the adverb that tells *how* an action happens. Circle the verb.

   a) She slowly walked to school.   **b)** The girls quickly got dressed.

4. Choose the correct pronoun to take the place of the noun naming people.

   a) Tell Mike. Tell _____. (he   him)   **b)** Show Elizabeth. Show _____. (she   her)

WEDNESDAY • Figures of Speech

Personification is giving human qualities or abilities to an animal or object.

Example: At exactly 6:30 a.m., <u>*my alarm clock sprang to life*</u>.
(Alarm clocks can't come alive.)

**1. Underline the animal or thing being personified in these sentences.
Circle what it is doing to show that it is an example of personification. Explain.**

a) Any hope I had left walked right out the door.

_____

b) The leaves danced in the wind.

_____

2. Put a check mark beside the sentence if it contains a simile.

She played with her hair as she talked. ___ The cat's eyes gleamed like diamonds. ___

THURSDAY • Vocabulary and Spelling

1. Write the contraction for each pair of words.

a) they will _____ (they've   they'll)

b) we had _____ (we'd   we've)

2. Fill in the blank with the correct word.

a) Sometimes I get _____ when I have nothing to do. (board   bored)

b) Are all passengers on _____ the train? (board   bored)

3. Correct the sentence for spelling. Rewrite the sentence.

We are goin shoping on Saterday.

_____

FRIDAY • Writing Prompt

A *recount* tells about events in the order that they happened.
Write a recount of an event of your choice. Draw the event.

☐ I told the order of events with words like first, next, then, before, after, and finally.

☐ I ordered my ideas in a way that makes sense.

☐ I used "I" or "we" in my writing.

☐ I made sure to include details that answer who, what, where, when, and why.

☐ I checked for correct spelling and punctuation.

MONDAY • Sentences and Punctuation

1. What is missing in the sentence fragment below? Circle the answer.

washed the laundry

(who or what is doing the action   the action   both are missing)

2. Rewrite the sentence fragment. Add what is missing to make a complete sentence.

_____

3. Add commas to separate the items in a series.

I play on a soccer team with Wyatt Andrew and Felix.

4. Use quotation marks around words that someone is speaking. Add quotation marks to each sentence.

a) Who took the last cupcake? Carlos asked.

b) This is the best pizza! exclaimed Abbie and Jacob.

TUESDAY • Grammar and Usage

Add an apostrophe and *s* to a singular noun to show possession.
Add just an apostrophe to a plural noun that ends with *s*.
Add an apostrophe and *s* to a plural noun that does *not* end with *s*.

1. Add an apostrophe or an apostrophe and *s* to form possessive nouns.

a) the teachers_____ classrooms   **b)** the fairies_____ wings

c) the pig_____ pen

2. Underline the verb in each sentence.

a) Two knights entered through the castle's main door.

b) The old farmer picks an apple from a low branch of the tree.

3. Circle all the adjectives in the sentence. Underline the noun each adjective describes. Draw an arrow from each adjective to the noun it describes.

An old car drove down the winding road on an early morning.

WEDNESDAY • Figures of Speech

1. *Onomatopoeia* is the use of a word that sounds like what it names. Think of something that makes this sound:

   a) Screech! _____   **b)** Roar! _____

2. Use the word list below to complete the oxymorons.

   hot   sweat   more   my   only

   a) cold _____   **b)** _____ choice

3. Write a sentence using one of the oxymorons.

   _____

4. Underline the animal or thing being personified in this sentence. Circle what it is doing to show that it is an example of personification.

   Light had finally conquered the darkness.

THURSDAY • Vocabulary and Spelling

1. Write the abbreviation for each word.

   a) Sunday _____   **b)** Wednesday _____   **c)** Monday _____

2. Circle the antonym for the bolded word.

   a) crooked   slash   straight   **b) dangerous**   threatening   safe

3. Circle the synonyms for the word *border*.

   edge   arms   boundary   margin   sort   perimeter

4. Read the sentence. Underline the word that has a prefix and a suffix.

   The back door was unlocked.

5. Complete the sentence by writing *to, two,* or *too*.

   My family is going _____ the school open house _____ .

FRIDAY • Writing Prompt

Draw a map from your school to where you live.

Title _____

Directions

_____

_____

_____

_____

_____

☐ My directions make sense.

☐ I used sequencing words like first, next, then and finally.

☐ I checked for correct spelling and punctuation.

☐ Challenge: I used the cardinal directions north, south, east and west.

MONDAY • Sentences and Punctuation

1. **For each sentence below, write *RO* if it is a run-on sentence. Put a check mark if the sentence is correct.**

    a) The lamp wasn't working, so I replaced the light bulb. _____

    b) Sydney was going to play tag with us she hurt her foot. _____

2. **Rewrite the sentence using correct capitalization and punctuation.**

    i am starving _____

Use quotation marks around words that someone is speaking. If the speaker tag comes before the spoken words, put a comma after the speaker tag.

   Example: The baker said, "This bread is very fresh."

3. **Add quotation marks and commas as necessary to the sentence.**

    The storekeeper announced We are closing in half an hour.

TUESDAY • Grammar and Usage

1. **Circle the correct verb.**

    a) A man and a woman with a baby (walk   walks) through the park.

    b) My brother or my sister often (helps   help) me with my homework.

2. **Change the *f* to a *v* and add *s* to make nouns ending with the letters *fe* plural.**

    a) knife _____   b) life _____   c) wife _____

3. **Write the article *a, an,* or *the* in each sentence.**

    a) When we go to the store, I always look at _____ sale items.

    b) Would you like _____ cup of tea and _____ almond cookie?

4. **Choose the best word to fill in the blank.**

    I did _____ on this spelling test than I did on the last one.   (better   best)

WEDNESDAY • Figures of Speech

1. *Idioms* are everyday phrases that mean something different from what they say. Although the phrase doesn't make literal sense, people understand its meaning. Match each idiom to its correct meaning.

Idiom	Meaning
slipped my mind	goes by fast
time flies	forgot
be all ears	good luck
break a leg	listen

2. Circle the words in the list that are examples of onomatopoeia.

kidding   rumble   boom   clash   glug   steal   cluck

3. Complete the simile.

   a) as cheap as a _____   **b)** cried like a _____

THURSDAY • Vocabulary and Spelling

1. Circle the words that have the sound of *long a.*
   Underline the words that have the sound of *short a.*

   aim   fame   cat   day   baby   flag   map

2. Write the contraction for each pair of words.

   a) does not _____ (doesn't   don't)

   b) should not _____ (shouldn't   should've)

3. Identify each pair of words as synonyms (S), antonyms (A), or homophones (H).

   a) four, fore _____   **b)** always, never _____   **c)** build, construct _____

4. Read the sentence. What does the word *convenient* mean?
   Circle the correct definition.

   Let's meet when it is most **_convenient_** for you.   (causing little effort or trouble   near)

FRIDAY • Writing Prompt

Persuasive writing gives your opinion and tries to convince the reader to agree with you.

Read the statement below. Write a persuasive paragraph to convince the reader of your opinion. Make sure to add details to support your thinking.

Our school should have longer recesses because...

First of all, _____

_____

_____

Another reason _____

_____

_____

Also, _____

_____

_____

This is why I think we should have longer _____

_____

☐ I clearly stated my opinion.

☐ I stated strong reasons and gave details.

☐ I organized my ideas in a way that makes sense.

☐ I used linking words to connect my ideas.

☐ I checked for correct spelling and punctuation.

MONDAY • Sentences and Punctuation

1. **Use quotation marks around words that someone is speaking. Add quotation marks and commas as necessary to each sentence.**

   a) Leanne exclaimed That was an amazing presentation!

   b) Ms. Finch said Please open your books to page 35.

2. **Write the correct punctuation mark at the end of each sentence. Name the sentence type.**

   a) The boys were playing softball at recess _____ _____

   b) Be careful _____ _____

3. **Add commas to separate the items in a series.**

   There are swings monkey bars and trapeze rings at the playground.

TUESDAY • Grammar and Usage

1. **Underline the verb in each sentence.**

   a) A reporter interviewed the new mayor after the election.

   b) Hamid records the main points of our discussion.

2. **Circle the correct verb.**

   a) Trucks or vans usually (park   parks) in the area behind the mall.

   b) Two deer and a fawn (walks   walk) silently through the forest.

3. **Underline the adverb that tells *where* an action happens.**

   a) Please leave the package here.   b) The frightened squirrel ran away.

4. **Write the correct pronoun to complete the sentence.**

   Can you please tell _____ what time is?   (I   me)

WEDNESDAY • Figures of Speech

1. Use the idiom in a sentence to show its correct meaning.

a) slipped my mind

_____

b) time flies

_____

2. Use the word list to complete the oxymoron.

bad   good   loud   silent   **a)** awfully _____   **b)** _____ scream

3. Underline the animal or thing being personified in this sentence. Circle what it is doing to show that it is an example of personification.

The old jalopy wheezed as it climbed the hill.

THURSDAY • Vocabulary and Spelling

1. Write the _prefix_, the _suffix_, and the _base word_.

Word	Prefix	Suffix	Base word
incorrectly			
refreshing			

2. Write the contraction for each pair of words.

a) I had _____ (I've   I'd)   **b)** you have _____ (you've   you'll)

c) they will _____ (they've   they'll)

3. Fill in the blank with the correct word.

a) When you add, you are finding the _____. (some   sum)

b) Would you like _____ fruit? (some   sum)

FRIDAY • Writing Prompt

A *cinquain* is a poem that has five lines.

Use the lines below to write cinquain poems about a person, place, or thing.

FORMAT

Line 1: two syllables

Line 2: four syllables

Line 3: six syllables

Line 4: eight syllables

Line 5: two syllables

FORMAT

Line 1: two syllables

Line 2: four syllables

Line 3: six syllables

Line 4: eight syllables

Line 5: two syllables

☐ I used interesting words.   ☐ I checked for correct spelling and punctuation.

MONDAY • Sentences and Punctuation

**1. Read the sentence. Circle the complete subject.
Underline the complete predicate.**

Our whole family went on a vacation to Banff National Park.

2. Change the statement to a command.

I put the knives, spoons, and forks in the drawer.

_____

**3. Use a comma after *yes* or *no* when it appears at the beginning of a sentence.
Add commas as necessary to each sentence.**

a) Yes I look forward to attending the party.   **b)** No I have not seen that movie.

**4. Use quotation marks around words that someone is speaking.
Add quotation marks and commas as necessary to the sentence.**

Dad warned Do not go near the construction site!

TUESDAY • Grammar and Usage

1. Circle the word in brackets that best completes the sentence.

The unexplored cave (might   must) be hiding a pirate's treasure.

2. Underline the common nouns and circle the proper nouns.

On Valentine's Day I bought chocolates for my teacher, Mrs. Alderson.

3. Choose the best pronoun to fill in the blank.

My brother and I did chores this morning.

_____ did chores this morning. (They   We)

4. Choose the best word to fill in the blank.

These oranges are the _____ I have had in a long time. (tastier   tastiest)

WEDNESDAY • Figures of Speech

1. Use each idiom in a sentence to show its correct meaning.

a) be all ears

_____

b) break a leg

_____

2. Complete the analogy.

short = _____   as   light = heavy

3. Finish the sentences using hyperbole.

a) This cat weighs a _____ !

b) Going on a school trip is the best idea _____ !

THURSDAY • Vocabulary and Spelling

1. Circle the antonym for the bolded word.

a) forget   remind   remember   **b) leader**   principal   follower

2. Circle the synonyms for the word _hurry_.

rush   shout   scurry   dash   speak

3. Complete the sentence by writing _their_, _there,_ or _they're_.

Lilly volunteered to feed _____ cat while _____ away.

4. What does _spell_ mean in this sentence? Circle the correct definition.

Professor Lee cast a **spell** on the snake.

(write or say letters of a word in the correct order   words that have magic powers)

FRIDAY • Writing Prompt

A *proverb* is a saying that offers some advice on how to live your life.

[ ]

1. a) Explain what you think the proverb below means. Draw the proverb.

"Every rose has its thorn."

_____

_____

b) Do you think this is good advice? Explain your thinking.

_____

_____

_____

_____

[ ] I checked for correct spelling.   [ ] I organized my ideas in a way that makes sense.

[ ] I checked for correct punctuation.   [ ] I used linking words to connect my ideas.

[ ] I used interesting words.   [ ] Challenge: I used a figure of speech.

MONDAY • Sentences and Punctuation

Use quotation marks around words that someone is speaking. When someone is speaking and says the name of the person they are speaking to, use a comma between the name and the rest of the sentence.

Examples: *"Tony, did you call me?" she asked.*

I replied, "I'm pleased to meet you, Mrs. Walker."

1. Add quotation marks and commas as necessary to each sentence.

a) Max can you come over on Saturday? Kyle asked.

b) Max answered I sure can Kyle.

2. What is missing in the sentence fragment below? Circle the answer.

inside my grandma's broom closet

(who or what is doing the action   the action   both are missing)

TUESDAY • Grammar and Usage

Add an apostrophe and *s* to a singular noun to show possession.
Add just an apostrophe to a plural noun that ends with *s*.
Add an apostrophe and *s* to a plural noun that does *not* end with *s*.

1. Add an apostrophe or an apostrophe and *s* to form possessive nouns.

a) my friend_____ parents   **b)** the deer_____ footprints   **c)** the bunnies_____ tails

2. Underline the verb in each sentence.

a) I illustrate my report with several maps and photos.

b) Our school choir performs three songs during the concert.

3. Make the nouns plural.

a) fish_____   **b)** person _____   **c)** glass_____

WEDNESDAY • Figures of Speech

1. Match each idiom to its correct meaning.

Idiom	Meaning
crack a book	be certain
in the bag	open a book and read

2. Is the book title an example of onomatopoeia? Circle YES or NO.

a) *Hop Up! Wriggle Over!*   **YES   NO**

b) *Why Mosquitoes Buzz in People's Ears*   **YES   NO**

c) *Wolf in the Snow*   **YES   NO**

d) *Click, Clack, Moo: Cows That Type*   **YES   NO**

THURSDAY • Vocabulary and Spelling

1. Write the *prefix*, the *suffix*, and the *base word*.

Word	Prefix	Suffix	Base word
misguided			
reforming			

2. Fill in the blank with the correct word.

a) The little puppy had the cutest _____ . (paws   pause)

b) There was a _____ before the teacher answered the question. (paws   pause)

3. Name the silent letter or letters in each word.

a) knee _____   b) crumb _____   c) like _____

4. How many syllables are there in the word *January*? _____

FRIDAY • Writing Prompt

**A *recount* tells about events in the order that they happened.
Write a recount of an event of your choice. Draw the event.**

_____

_____

_____

_____

_____

_____

☐ I told the order of events with words like first, next, then, before, after, and finally.

☐ I ordered my ideas in a way that makes sense.

☐ I used "I" or "we" in my writing.

☐ I made sure to include details that answer who, what, where, when, and why.

☐ I checked for correct spelling and punctuation.

MONDAY • Sentences and Punctuation

1. Fill in the blank with the correct conjunction.

   a) We can have hamburgers for dinner, _____ we can have pizza.   (or so)

   b) The restaurant did not have hamburgers, _____ we got pizza.   (or so)

2. Add commas to separate the things in a series.

We had salad meatloaf and potatoes for dinner.

3. Add quotation marks and commas as necessary to each sentence.

   a) Mrs Mendez said Holly are you able to babysit this afternoon?

   b) Holly responded No I am sorry.

4. Write an example of a sentence that is a command.

TUESDAY • Grammar and Usage

1. Complete the sentence by writing the past tense of the verb in brackets.

   a) Marcus _____ (spend) all his money at the fair.

   b) Last year, I _____ (read) five books during summer vacation.

2. Circle the word in brackets that best completes the sentence.

   a) When I was a baby, my mother (could   would   will) sing me lullabies.

   b) (May   Should   Must) I please invite a friend to dinner?

3. Underline the adverb that tells *how often* an action happens.

   a) My grandmother always gives me hugs.

   b) I got locked out twice in a week.

WEDNESDAY • Figures of Speech

1. Use each idiom in a sentence to show its correct meaning.

a) crack a book

_____

b) in the bag

_____

2. Use a word from the list to complete the oxymoron.

great   awful   time   hour   thief   person

a) endless _____   **b)** honest _____

3. Finish the sentence using alliteration.

Jolly _____ jumped and ate _____ .

THURSDAY • Vocabulary and Spelling

1. Identify each pair of words as synonyms (S), antonyms (A), or homophones (H).

a) add, total _____   **b)** not, knot _____   **c)** brave, cowardly _____

2. Write the abbreviation for each word.

a) street _____   **b)** June _____   **c)** doctor _____

3. Write the contraction for each pair of words.

a) they had _____ (they'll   they'd)   **b)** we have _____ (we'd   we've)

4. Spell this word correctly:

carryed _____

5. Underline the phrase that has a negative connotation.

a) complain about this   talk about this   **b)** close the door   slam the door

FRIDAY • Writing Prompt

A *fact* is information that can be *proven* to be true. An *opinion* is a statement based on something a person *thinks* or *believes* to be true.

Fill in the table with two examples of facts and two examples of opinion.

Statement	Fact or Opinion	How do you know? Explain your thinking.

MONDAY • Sentences and Punctuation

1. For each sentence below, write RO if it is a run-on sentence. Put a check mark if the sentence is correct.

a) Mike threw the ball it went over the fence. _____

b) I need an umbrella it is raining outside. _____

2. Write the correct punctuation mark at the end of each sentence. Name the sentence type.

a) When is your doctor's appointment _____   _____

b) Go to sleep _____   _____

3. Add commas to separate the items in a series.

The parent council includes parents teachers and the principal.

TUESDAY • Grammar and Usage

**The main verb in a sentence tells the action.
Usually, a helping verb comes before the main verb.**

*Example: Chris will **sweep** the kitchen floor.*

The main verb is "sweep." The helping verb is "will."

1. Circle the main verb and underline the helping verb.

My brother and sister were watching a nature show.

2. Use one of the pronouns below to complete each sentence.

myself   yourself   herself   himself   itself   yourselves   ourselves   themselves

a) I could ask someone to fix my bike, but I'll try to do it _____.

b) My little sister likes to look at _____ in the mirror.

WEDNESDAY • Figures of Speech

1. a) Underline the two things compared in the metaphor.

The highway was a parking lot.

b) Explain the metaphor in your own words.

_____

2. Is the book title an example of alliteration? Circle YES or NO.

a) *Black Beauty*   YES   NO   **b)** *A Very Hungry Caterpillar*   YES   NO

c) *Peter Pan*   YES   NO   **d)** *Doctor Doolittle*   YES   NO

3. Complete the analogy. Think about what the two things have in common.

strawberry = _____   as   blueberry = _____

THURSDAY • Vocabulary and Spelling

1. Identify the word pairs as synonyms or antonyms.

a) idea, plan _____   **b)** injure, heal _____

c) show, hide _____   **d)** kind, type _____

2. Complete the table. Use each new word in a sentence to show its meaning.

Base word	Add the prefix	Add the suffix	New word
expect	*un*	*ed*	
cover	*re*	*ing*	

_____

3. Circle the word that *does not* belong in the group.

hold   clutch   drop   grip

FRIDAY • Writing Prompt

Persuasive writing gives your opinion and tries to convince the reader to agree with you.

Read the statement below. Write a persuasive paragraph to convince the reader of your opinion. Make sure to add details to support your thinking.

"Students should have homework every day."

I (agree, disagree) that children should have homework every day.

_____

_____

_____

_____

_____

_____

_____

This is why I think _____ .

☐ I clearly stated my opinion.

☐ I stated strong reasons and gave details.

☐ I organized my ideas in a way that makes sense.

☐ I used linking words to connect my ideas.

☐ I checked for correct spelling and punctuation.

MONDAY • Sentences and Punctuation

1. Read the sentence. Circle the complete subject. Underline the complete predicate.

The rude student interrupted the teacher.

**2. For each sentence below, write *RO* if it is a run-on sentence.
Put a check mark if the sentence is correct.**

a) The toys are outside they need to come in. _____

b) My sister washed the clothes and I folded them. _____

3. Write an example of a sentence that is a question.

_____

4. Add quotation marks and commas as necessary to each sentence.

a) Samantha yelled Simon you cheated!

b) Why do I always have to take out the garbage? complained Kim.

TUESDAY • Grammar and Usage

1. Write the possessive form of the noun in brackets.

a) After fishing, the _____ (fishermen) nets were full of fish.

b) A _____ (branch) leaves turn colour in the fall.

2. Underline the verb in each sentence.

a) We surveyed students in the school about their hobbies.

b) Alicia, our group leader, suggests some possible solutions to the problem.

**3. Underline the adjectives in the sentence.
Circle whether each adjective is before or after the noun.**

The wild flowers swayed in the soft breeze.   (before   after)

WEDNESDAY • Figures of Speech

1. Fill in the blanks with onomatopoeic words.

a) The big rock made a loud _____ when it hit the dirt.

b) My cousin can _____ loudly after drinking pop.

2. Circle the examples of oxymorons.

found missing   mud bath   wasted time   oven fried

3. Make up a simile and use it in a sentence.

_____

4. Underline the animal or thing being personified in this sentence.
Circle what it is doing to show that it is an example of personification.

The lunch she ate did not agree with her.

THURSDAY • Vocabulary and Spelling

1. Fill in the blank with the correct word.

a) The _____ galloped in the field.   (horse   hoarse)

b) Ava's voice was a _____ whisper.   (horse   hoarse)

2 Circle the word that *does not* belong in the group.

hammer   saw   screwdriver   boots

3. Complete the sentence with the best prefix.

a) Remember to _____ heat the oven before baking.   (pre   un)

b) I need to _____ turn my library books tomorrow.   (mis   re)

4. Make three compound words using these words: tooth fish cut hair star brush

_____   _____   _____

FRIDAY • Writing Prompt

A *Diamond* poem is a poem that makes the shape of a diamond.

Choose a person, place, or thing and write a Diamond poem using nouns, adjectives, and verbs.

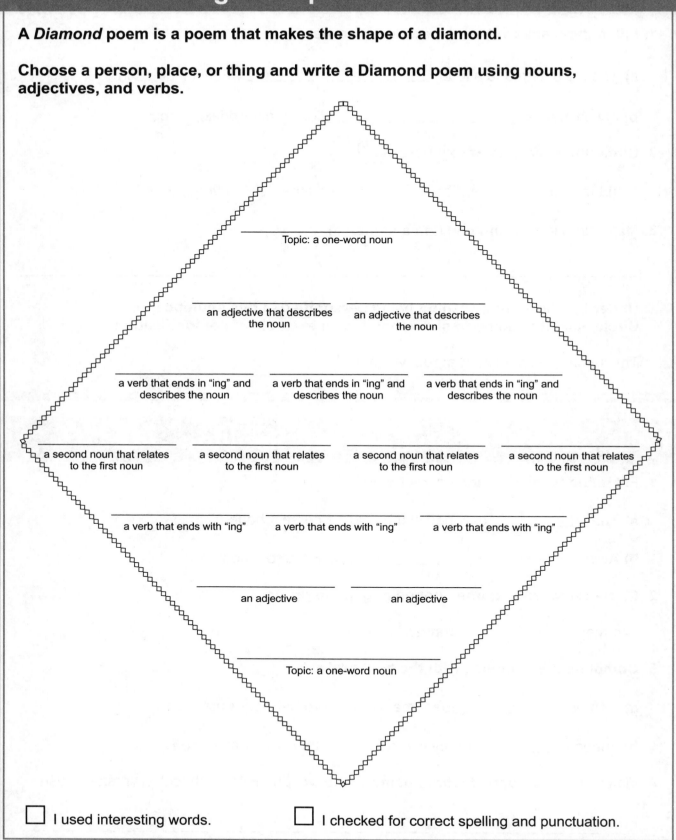

_____
Topic: a one-word noun

_____   _____
an adjective that describes   an adjective that describes
the noun   the noun

_____   _____   _____
a verb that ends in "ing" and   a verb that ends in "ing" and   a verb that ends in "ing" and
describes the noun   describes the noun   describes the noun

_____   _____   _____   _____
a second noun that relates   a second noun that relates   a second noun that relates   a second noun that relates
to the first noun   to the first noun   to the first noun   to the first noun

_____   _____   _____
a verb that ends with "ing"   a verb that ends with "ing"   a verb that ends with "ing"

_____   _____
an adjective   an adjective

_____
Topic: a one-word noun

☐ I used interesting words.   ☐ I checked for correct spelling and punctuation.

MONDAY • Sentences and Punctuation

1. Fill in the blank with the best conjunction.

I was walking to school _____ it started to snow.   (since   when)

2. Use a comma after *yes* or *no* when it appears at the beginning of a sentence.

a) Yes I had a visit with my aunt and uncle.

b) No you cannot go to the store.

3. Add a complete subject to make this a sentence.

_____ watched the dolphin at the aquarium.

4. Correct and rewrite the sentence.

Yes I had heard that dr. gotti is moving to brandon Manitoba in september?

_____

TUESDAY • Grammar and Usage

1. Complete the sentence by writing the past tense of the verb in brackets.

a) The woman _____ (keep) her jewels locked up in a safe.

b) The days _____ (become) shorter as winter approached.

2. Circle the word in brackets that best completes the sentence.

a) You (may   should   might) be very careful when crossing this busy street.

b) You (could   would) play a video game if you're bored this afternoon.

3. Make the nouns plural.
For some nouns that end in *o*, add the letters *es* to make them plural.
For other nouns that end in *o*, just add *s* to make them plural.

a) echo_____   **b)** potato _____   **c)** zero _____

WEDNESDAY • Figures of Speech

1. Match each idiom to its correct meaning.

Idiom	Meaning
to get cold feet	to be cranky
to get up on the wrong side of the bed	to get nervous

2. *Onomatopoeia* **is the use of a word that sounds like what it names. Think of something that makes this sound:**

a) Oink! _____   **b)** Tick! Tock! _____

3. a) Underline the oxymoron in the sentence.

Her messy chocolate cake was disgustingly delicious.

b) Explain the meaning of the oxymoron.

_____

THURSDAY • Vocabulary and Spelling

1. Complete the sentence by writing *to, two,* **or** *too*.

My family is going _____ the concert _____ .

2. Write the contraction for each pair of words.

a) she had _____ (she'd   she'll)   **b)** he will _____ (he'll   he'd)

3. Circle the correct spelling for the plural form of the word *goose*.

geese   gease   geece

4. What is a word that has two syllables? _____

5. List the abbreviations for the words below.

centimetres _____   kilometres _____   millimetres _____

FRIDAY • Writing Prompt

If you could be any age, what would it be? Draw and write about it.

☐ I checked for correct spelling.   ☐ I organized my ideas in a way that makes sense.

☐ I checked for correct punctuation. ☐ I used linking words to connect my ideas.

☐ I used interesting words.   ☐ Challenge: I used a figure of speech.

MONDAY • Sentences and Punctuation

1. What is missing in the sentence fragment below? Circle the answer.

on the kitchen table

(who or what is doing the action   the action   both are missing)

2. Rewrite the sentence fragment. Add what is missing to make a complete sentence.

_____

3. Add commas to separate the items in a series.

My favourite fruits are bananas pineapples and oranges.

4. Unscramble these words to make a sentence that is a statement. Add capitals as needed.

halifax the capital of is nova Scotia.

_____

TUESDAY • Grammar and Usage

**The *main verb* in a sentence tells the action.
Usually, a helping verb comes before the main verb.**

*Example: Flags <u>were</u> **flapping** in the wind.*

The main verb is "flapping." The helping verb is "were."

1. Circle the main verb and underline the helping verb.

Marina has told me about her trip to Italy.

2. Underline the common nouns and circle the proper nouns.

Dr. Garret has an office in a building on Oxford Street in London, Ontario.

3. Choose the correct pronoun to complete the sentence.

Come with _____ to the movies.   (we   us)

WEDNESDAY • Figures of Speech

1. **Use each idiom in a sentence to show its correct meaning.**

   a) get cold feet

   _____

   b) get up on the wrong side of the bed

   _____

2. **Complete the analogy.**

   scent = _____ as sound = ear

3. **Finish the sentence using alliteration.**

   Silly _____ saw some _____ .

THURSDAY • Vocabulary and Spelling

1. **Read the pair of words. Circle the sound you hear in each word.**

   a) race cat soft c hard c   **b)** large gate soft g hard g

2. **Complete the table. Use the new word in a sentence to show its meaning.**

Base word	Add the prefix	Add the suffix	New word
event	_un_	_ful_	

   _____

3. **Which word means _something_ you win? Circle the answer.** (prize gift)

4. **Correct and rewrite the sentence.**

   In Joone, dr. Sotto will travel to winipeg.

   _____

FRIDAY • Writing Prompt

A *proverb* is a saying that offers some advice on how to live your life.

[blank box]

1. a) Explain what you think the proverb below means. Draw the saying.

"A leopard does not change its spots."

_____

_____

b) Do you think this is good advice? Explain your thinking.

_____

_____

_____

_____

☐ I checked for correct spelling.   ☐ I organized my ideas in a way that makes sense.

☐ I checked for correct punctuation.   ☐ I used linking words to connect my ideas.

☐ I used interesting words.   ☐ Challenge: I used a figure of speech.

MONDAY • Sentences and Punctuation

1. Fill in the blank with the correct conjunction.

I played a video game _____ I had to get ready for dinner.   (until   because)

2. Finish the sentence by adding a complete predicate.

There was a strange person _____ .

3. Unscramble these words to make a command sentence.

what me do tell do to not

_____

Add quotation marks and commas as necessary to each sentence.

a) Jacques yelled Be careful!

b) Where can I find a pencil sharpener? asked Dmitri.

TUESDAY • Grammar and Usage

1. Circle the correct verb.

The workers and their supervisor (meet   meets) to discuss the new rules.

2. Is the word *slice* a noun or a verb? Circle the answer.

a) I need to slice the vegetables for the salad.   (noun   verb)

b) I would love a slice of coconut cream pie.   (noun   verb)

3. Write the correct form of the verb in brackets to make the pronoun and verb agree.

They _____ to the top of the mountain this afternoon.   (hikes   hike)

4. Circle all the adjectives in the sentence. Underline the noun each adjective describes. Draw an arrow from each adjective to the noun it describes.

It was a warm day with many children playing in the school playground.

WEDNESDAY • Figures of Speech

1. a) **Underline the oxymoron in the sentence.**

   Canned peas are my least favourite food.

   b) **Explain the meaning of the oxymoron.**

   _____

2. a) **Underline the two things compared in the metaphor.**

   Books are the keys to the imagination.

   b) **Explain the metaphor in your own words.**

   _____

3. **Write an example of alliteration using the letter *M*.**

   _____

THURSDAY • Vocabulary and Spelling

1. **Write the abbreviation for each word.**

   a) February _____   b) Mister _____   c) Ontario _____

2. **Choose a *synonym* for the word in brackets. Write the word in the blank.**

   chomp   danger   forbidden   sick   sleepy

   a) The sign said, " _____ ! Deep water here." (hazard)

   b) Minnie took homemade chicken soup to her _____ aunt.   (ailing)

3. **Underline the *antonym* for the bolded word.**

   a) **absent**   present   late

   b) **fail**   trip   succeed

FRIDAY • Writing Prompt

A *recount* tells about events in the order that they happened.
Write a recount of an event of your choice. Draw the event.

_____

_____

_____

_____

_____

_____

- [ ] I told the order of events with words like first, next, then, before, after, and finally.
- [ ] I ordered my ideas in a way that makes sense.
- [ ] I used "I" or "we" in my writing.
- [ ] I made sure to include details that answer who, what, where, when, and why.
- [ ] I checked for correct spelling and punctuation.

MONDAY • Sentences and Punctuation

1. Read the sentence. Circle the complete subject. Underline the complete predicate.

Ben's older brother plays on the basketball team.

2. Write the correct punctuation mark at the end of each sentence. Name the sentence type.

a) This is the best book I have ever read _____   _____

b) Get ready for bed _____   _____

3. Write a statement telling the name of the hospital closest to you.

_____

4. Correct and rewrite the sentence.

i needs a pencil an eraser paper and a place to do homework

_____

TUESDAY • Grammar and Usage

1. Write the possessive form of the noun.

a) A glass of water fell on the book. The book_____ pages got wet.

b) The boxers_____ gloves hung in the locker room.

2. Underline the verb in each sentence.

a) The company's president interrupted the meeting with some important news.

b) This unfriendly dog always growls at strangers.

3. Choose the correct pronoun to complete the sentence.

Have _____ gone to the new art museum?   (you   them)

4. Choose the correct preposition from the words in brackets.

I hope we are going to the beach _____ Sunday.   (with   on)

WEDNESDAY • Figures of Speech

1. Match each idiom to its correct meaning.

Idiom

a long shot

to be sick as a dog

Meaning

to feel really sick

a small possibility

2. a) Underline the animal or thing being personified in this sentence. Circle what it is doing to show that it is an example of personification.

The school looked sad after the students left for the summer.

b) Explain your thinking.

_____

3. Fill in the blank using hyperbole to make the sentence more exaggerated.

I have a _____ of chores to finish.

THURSDAY • Vocabulary and Spelling

1. Circle the words that have the sound of *long u*. Underline the words that have the sound of *short u*.

huge   few   tube   bug   cute   sun

2. What is the abbreviation for the month in which you were born? _____

3. Circle the contraction in each sentence. Write the words that form the contraction.

a) I'm going to the grocery store. _____

b) They're planning a celebration dinner. _____

4. Underline the phrase that is more positive.

a) Ravi was thrilled about getting a puppy.

b) Ravi was glad to be going to his uncle's house.

FRIDAY • Writing Prompt

A *procedure* is a set of numbered steps to follow to make or do something. **Write a procedure for something that is easy to make or do. Write a recipe for a magical potion.**

Describe the purpose of the magical potion.

_____

Special Ingredients

_____

_____

_____

Instructions

_____

_____

_____

_____

_____

_____

☐ I have a description that tells what you will make or do.

☐ The information is organized under headings.

☐ Each step has a number.

☐ I used action words to tell which actions to do.

☐ I checked for correct spelling and punctuation.

MONDAY • Sentences and Punctuation

1. Fill in the blank with the best conjunction.

I had breakfast _____ I got dressed.   (before   after)

2. Add commas to separate the items in a series.

The recipe calls for milk flour butter and eggs.

3. Add quotation marks and commas as necessary to the sentence.

Janelle asked What time do we need to leave?

4. Unscramble these words to make a sentence that is an exclamation.

the I worst ever meal this eaten is have

_____

TUESDAY • Grammar and Usage

1. Complete the sentence by writing the past tense of the verb in brackets.

a) The hot air balloon slowly _____ (rise) into the sky.

b) The Walkers _____ (choose) blue drapes for their living room.

2. Write the correct pronoun to complete the sentence.

a) Can _____ help you?   (I   me)

3. Write a sentence that includes an adverb that tells *where* an action happens.

_____

4. Use the correct form of the adjective in brackets. Write it on the line.

My piece of cake is _____ (small) than your piece.

WEDNESDAY • Figures of Speech

1. **Use each idiom in a sentence to show its correct meaning.**

   a) a long shot

   _____

   b) be sick as a dog

   _____

2. **Is this an example of alliteration? Circle YES or NO.**

   a) Ten tiny turtles talked on the telephone.   **YES   NO**

   b) Cats often run around the house at night.   **YES   NO**

3. **Make up a simile and use it in a sentence.**

   _____

THURSDAY • Vocabulary and Spelling

1. **Complete the sentence by writing *their*, *there*, or *they're*.**

   Where are _____ coats?

2. **Write the contraction for each pair of words.**

   a) she will _____ (she's   she'll)   **b)** he had _____ (he'll   he'd)

3. **Circle the correct spelling for the plural form of the word *mouse*.**

   mise   mice   myce

4. **Fill in the blank with the correct word.**

   a) There is a stainless _____ sink in our kitchen.   (steal   steel)

   b) The jewel thief tried to _____ the necklace.   (steal   steel)

5. **What is a word that has four syllables?** _____

FRIDAY • Writing Prompt

Persuasive writing gives your opinion and tries to convince the reader to agree with you.

Read the statement below. Write a persuasive paragraph to convince the reader of your argument. Make sure to add details to support your thinking.

"Do cats or dogs make a better pet?"

I think a (cat, dog) makes a better pet because...

_____

_____

_____

_____

_____

_____

_____

This is why I think _____
.

☐ I clearly stated my opinion.

☐ I stated strong reasons and gave details.

☐ I organized my ideas in a way that makes sense.

☐ I used linking words to connect my ideas.

☐ I checked for correct spelling and punctuation.

MONDAY • Sentences and Punctuation

1. For each sentence below, write *RO* if it is a run-on sentence. Put a check mark if the sentence is correct.

a) You like strawberries I prefer mangoes. ____

b) Because it was so hot we decided to go swimming. ____

2. Add quotation marks and commas as needed.

a) I can't wait for the field trip! exclaimed Jaffir.

b) Tao we are so excited to come and see you in the school play said Mom and Dad.

3. Finish the sentence by adding a complete subject.

_____ was stuck in traffic.

TUESDAY • Grammar and Usage

The *main* verb in a sentence tells the action. Usually, a helping verb comes before the main verb.

*Example: The snow <u>has</u> **melted** in the warm sun.*

The main verb is "melted." The helping verb is "has."

1. Circle the main verb and underline the helping verb.

a) Today, I am going to the grocery store with my dad.

b) I was running a little late for my appointment yesterday.

2. Underline the common nouns and circle the proper nouns.

My cousin Mary goes to Fancy Footwear every Boxing Day to buy shoes and sandals.

3. Write a sentence that includes an adverb that tells *when* an action happens.

_____

WEDNESDAY • Figures of Speech

1. a) Underline the animal or thing being personified in this sentence. Circle what it is doing to show that it is an example of personification.

As we built sandcastles on the beach, the sun beat down on us.

b) Explain your thinking.

_____

2. Fill in the blanks with onomatopoeic words.   splash   hiss   squirt

a) The rock made a big _____ when Jan threw it in the pond.

b) When Mia squeezed the tube, the toothpaste _____ out.

3. Underline the two things compared in the metaphor.

Her voice was music to his ears.

THURSDAY • Vocabulary and Spelling

1. Circle the meaning of the underlined word.

At our team <u>banquet</u> we had a delicious meal and gave out awards.

(a meeting   a celebration meal)

2. Write the contraction for each pair of words.

a) could not _____ (couldn't   can't)

b) would not _____ (won't   wouldn't)

3. Complete the sentence with the correct prefix.

a) I made a _____ take on my spelling test. (mis   un)

b) The crystal was _____ like any other I had seen. (un   re)

4. Write two words that rhyme with *pool*. _____

FRIDAY • Writing Prompt

Draw a picture and write the text for a missing object or pet.

LOST!

Who or What? _____

Why? _____

Reward _____   Please call _____

Description

_____

_____

_____

_____

☐ My writing makes sense.   ☐ I used decriptive words and phrases.

☐ I checked for correct spelling.   ☐ I checked for correct capitalization
                                       and punctuation.

MONDAY • Sentences and Punctuation

1. **Fill in the blank with the correct conjunction.**

   My sister checked her email _____ she got home. (as soon as   while)

2. **What is missing in the sentence fragment below? Circle the answer.**

   moving quickly along the path

   (who or what is doing the action   the action   both are missing)

3. **Rewrite the sentence fragment. Add what is missing to make a complete sentence.**

   _____

4. **Correct the run-on sentence by writing it as two sentences.**

   The girl opened the book she read it in the cozy chair.

   _____

TUESDAY • Grammar and Usage

1. **Circle the word in brackets that best completes the sentence.**

   a) (Could   Should   Will) a rabbit have eaten the lettuce in the garden?

   b) If I were you, I (may   would   must) apologize for losing my temper.

2. **Circle the correct verb.**

   a) My mother or my father (drive   drives) me to baseball practice.

   b) Two ambulances and a fire truck (rushes   rush) to the burning building.

3. **Rewrite the sentence to make the underlined nouns plural.**
   Do not use the words *a* or *an* before a plural noun.

   The **child** watched a **video** and played a **game**.

   _____

WEDNESDAY • Figures of Speech

1. **a) Underline the oxymoron in the sentence.**

   The look on his face showed he was clearly confused.

   b) Explain the meaning of the oxymoron.

   _____

2. **Complete the analogy.**

   cucumber = _____   as   pumpkin = orange

3. **a) Underline the two things compared in the metaphor.**

   Laughter is the best medicine.

   b) Explain the metaphor in your own words.

   _____

THURSDAY • Vocabulary and Spelling

1. **Name the silent letter or letters in each word.**

   a) whale _____   **b)** high _____   **c)** whistle _____

2. **Write the contraction for each pair of words.**

   a) we will _____ (we've   we'll)   **b)** you will _____ (you'd   you'll)

3. **Identify each word pair as synonyms or antonyms.**

   a) gift, present _____

   b) artificial, natural _____

   c) spare, extra _____

   d) repair, destroy _____

4. **How many syllables are there in the word *imagination*?** _____

FRIDAY • Writing Prompt

Would you rather travel back in time or into the future? Draw your adventure. Explain your reasons.

☐ I checked for correct spelling.   ☐ I organized my ideas in a way that makes sense.

☐ I checked for correct punctuation.   ☐ I used linking words to connect my ideas.

☐ I used interesting words.   ☐ Challenge: I used a figure of speech.

MONDAY • Sentences and Punctuation

1. Read the sentence. Circle the complete subject. Underline the complete predicate.

The laughing children tracked mud as they came inside the house.

2. Write the correct punctuation mark at the end of each sentence. Name the sentence type.

a) I had a sandwich, an apple, and some milk for lunch _____   _____

b) When did you receive your invitation _____   _____

3. Add commas to separate the items in a series.

Please pick up eggs bread and cheese at the grocery store.

4. Choose the correct verb to make the subject and verb agree.

I _____ Sal and Marco over to see our new puppy.   (calls called)

TUESDAY • Grammar and Usage

1. Complete the sentence by writing the past tense of the verb in brackets.

a) The children _____ (build) sandcastles on the beach.

b) Roger _____ (feel) sorry for the lost puppy.

2. Rewrite the sentence. Use a plural pronoun to replace the underlined phrase.

My friend and I went to the library.

_____

3. Choose the correct preposition from the words in brackets.

I am bringing nacho chips _____ the class party.   (for in)

4. Write *more* or *most* to complete the sentence correctly.

Your lasagna is the _____ delicious I have ever had.

WEDNESDAY • Figures of Speech

1. Write an example of alliteration using the letter *S*.

_____

2. a) Complete the simile.

as slimy as _____

b) Use the simile in a sentence.

_____

3. a) Underline the two things compared in the metaphor.

Bruno's temper was a volcano.

b) Explain the metaphor in your own words.

_____

THURSDAY • Vocabulary and Spelling

1. Write the abbreviation for each word.

a) Junior _____

b) Avenue _____

c) Boulevard _____

2. Think of a synonym for the word in brackets. Write the word in the blank.

a) I made only one _____ on my math test!   (error)

b) Salma was in a _____ to get to her music class.   (hurry)

3. Fill in the blank with the correct word.

a) I am so hungry I could eat the _____ pie! (hole   whole)

b) The brown gopher disappeared down the _____ in the ground. (hole   whole)

FRIDAY • Writing Prompt

Create a new expression that people can use as advice in their daily lives. Draw and write about the saying.

1. a) What is your new saying?

_____

b) Explain what it means.

_____

_____

c) How does it relate to your life?

_____

_____

_____

_____

☐ I checked for correct spelling.   ☐ I organized my ideas in a way that makes sense.

☐ I checked for correct punctuation.   ☐ I used linking words to connect my ideas.

☐ I used interesting words.   ☐ Challenge: I used a figure of speech.

 Canadian Daily Language Skills, Grade 4 © Chalkboard Publishing Inc.

MONDAY • Sentences and Punctuation

1. Use a comma after *yes* or *no* when it appears at the beginning of a sentence.

   a) Yes I would like another helping of pie.

   b) No I am leaving in the morning.

2. Fill in the blank with the best conjunction.

   We ate popcorn _____ we watched the movie.   (because   while)

3. Add quotation marks and commas as necessary to the sentence.

   Alex would you like to share your story with the class? Mrs. Turnbull asked.

4. Rewrite the sentence using correct capitalization and punctuation.

   is it true that valentine's day is morgans favourite holiday

   _____

TUESDAY • Grammar and Usage

1. Circle the main verb and underline the helping verb.

   a) How many people are swimming in the pool?

   b) The leaky tap was dripping all night long.

2. Underline the common nouns and circle the proper nouns.

   Harry's Burger Bar in Clearview Mall makes amazing burgers, fries, and milkshakes.

3. Write the correct pronoun to complete the sentence.

   My friend and _____ are in the same class.   (I   me)

4. Does the adjective in the sentence tell *what kind* or *how many*?

   The helpful students cleaned up the classroom. _____

WEDNESDAY • Figures of Speech

**1. a) Underline the animal or thing being personified in this sentence.
Circle what it is doing to show that it is an example of personification.**

The hockey puck flew past the goalie into the net.

b) Explain your thinking.

_____

2. Fill in the blank using hyperbole to make the sentence more exaggerated.

a) This ice cream cone is _____ .

b) It is so cold in this room that _____ .

THURSDAY • Vocabulary and Spelling

**1. Circle the words that have the sound of *long i.*
Underline the words that have the sound of *short i.***

shine   fit   night   cry   milk

2. List a synonym for the word *fast.* _____

3. List an antonym for the word *quiet.* _____

4. How many syllables does this word have?   unusual   _____

**5. The word *show* can have more than one meaning.
Write a sentence to show two meanings of the word *show.***

_____

FRIDAY • Writing Prompt

A *recount* tells about events in the order that they happened. Pretend you just saw an alien from space land and in your backyard. Write a recount of what you saw. Draw the event.

_____

_____

_____

_____

_____

_____

☐ I told the order of events with words like first, next, then, before, after, and finally.

☐ I ordered my ideas in a way that makes sense.

☐ I used "I" or "we" in my writing.

☐ I made sure to include details that answer who, what, where, when, and why.

☐ I checked for correct spelling and punctuation.

MONDAY • Sentences and Punctuation

1. Add quotation marks and commas as necessary to each sentence.

a) monster reunion is the funniest movie ever exclaimed Eva

b) watch for that car yelled tommy

2. Fill in the blank with the correct conjunction.

My friend needs to go home soon _____ her family has company over.
(after   because)

3. Unscramble these words to make a sentence that is a command.

vegetables   now   eat   your

_____

TUESDAY • Grammar and Usage

1. In each sentence, circle the correct possessive form of the noun in brackets.

a) The two (team's   teams') uniforms were ready in the change rooms.

b) I tried two markers, but both (markers'   markers's) ink had run out.

2. Circle the correct verb.

a) The store manager or a salesperson (lock   locks) the door at closing time.

b) Two spoons and a fork (falls   fall) to the floor.

3. Replace the underlined word with the correct pronoun.

a) <u>Him</u> moved to Alberta. _____   b) <u>Us</u> are going to visit him. _____

4. Write a sentence that includes two adjectives.

_____

WEDNESDAY • Figures of Speech

1. Match each idiom to its correct meaning.

Idiom	Meaning
zip your lip	very happy
over the moon	be very quiet

2. Write an example of alliteration using the letter _D_.

_____

3. Underline the two things compared in the metaphor.

a) My grandma's dog is a stubborn mule.

b) Her tears were a river flowing down her face.

4. Use the oxymoron in a sentence to show its meaning.   act naturally

_____

THURSDAY • Vocabulary and Spelling

1. Complete the sentence by writing _to, two,_ or _too_.

Our _____ dogs are coming with us _____ the park.

2. Write the contraction for each pair of words.

a) is not _____ (it's   isn't)   **b)** it is _____ (its   it's)

3. Circle the word or phrase that sound more negative.

a) open rip   **b)** slip slap   **c)** walked away ran off

4. Correct the sentence for spelling mistakes. Rewrite the sentence.

They're house is on the same streat as my cuzzin's.

_____

FRIDAY • Writing Prompt

Write a *review*. Share your opinion about a book or movie.

Title: _____

Description:

_____

_____

_____

In my opinion:

_____

_____

_____

_____

_____

_____

_____

☐ My writing makes sense.
☐ I used interesting words.

☐ I used linking words to connect my ideas.
☐ I checked for correct spelling and punctuation.

MONDAY • Sentences and Punctuation

1. Read the sentence. Circle the complete subject. Underline the complete predicate.

My baby brother broke my remote-controlled car.

2. Write the correct punctuation mark at the end of each sentence. Name the sentence type.

a) That is disgusting ____   _____

b) I don't understand the question ____   _____

3. Add commas to separate the items in a series.

I need sunglasses sunscreen and a sun hat for the beach.

4. Rewrite the sentence to make the subject and verb agree.

Mr. Tanaka give out homework every Friday afternoon.

_____

TUESDAY • Grammar and Usage

1. Circle the main verb and underline the helping verb.

a) The students have discussed their ideas in groups.

b) The volcano will erupt soon, according to scientists.

2. Write the correct form of the verb in brackets to make the pronoun and verb agree.

We _____ to my cousin's cottage next week. (travels)

3. Write the article *a, an,* or *the* in the sentence.

_____ secretary at our school always has ____ pencil and ____ eraser handy.

4. Write a sentence that includes an adverb that tells *how often* an action happens.

_____

WEDNESDAY • Figures of Speech

1. **Read the sentence. Identify the figure of speech.**

   a) He tried to run away, but his legs were rubber.   (metaphor   hyperbole)

   b) This book is as boring as watching paint dry!   (metaphor   hyperbole)

2. **Use each idiom in a sentence to show its correct meaning.**

   a) zip your lip

   _____

   b) over the moon

   _____

3. **Complete the simile.**

   The traffic jam was like a _____

THURSDAY • Vocabulary and Spelling

1. **Circle the meaning of the underlined word.**

   The people were very upset after they heard the <u>tragic</u> news.

   (terrible or awful   huge or big)

2. **Fill in the blank with the correct word.**

   a) I have _____ this long blue dress before.   (worn   warn)

   b) The police came to _____ people of the danger.   (worn   warn)

3. **Which of these words have the same base word as circle?**

   circulate   cycle   circus

FRIDAY • Writing Prompt

Design a restaurant menu! First, choose foods for your menu. Then, write a detailed description for each menu item. Use interesting words to make customers' mouths water.

Restaurant Name _____

This restaurant is known for _____

Starters

_____

_____

Main Courses

_____

_____

_____

_____

Dessert Specials

_____

_____

Drinks

_____

_____

☐ My writing makes sense.

☐ My descriptions will make people want to order the food.

☐ I checked for correct spelling and punctuation.

MONDAY • Sentences and Punctuation

1. Add quotation marks and all the correct punctuation to each sentence.

a) Have you seen my bike Debbie asked John

b) Fetch the stick Mom said to our dog

2. Fill in the blank with the correct conjunction.

I picked up some batteries _____ I was already at the store.   (since   when)

3. What is missing in the sentence fragment below? Circle the answer.

singing loudly

(who or what is doing the action   the action   both are missing)

4. Rewrite the sentence fragment. Add what is missing to make a complete sentence.

_____

TUESDAY • Grammar and Usage

1. Complete the sentence by writing the past tense of the verb in brackets.

a) The principal _____ (speak) to the students about bullying.

b) The woman _____ (pay) for her groceries with a credit card.

2. Circle the word in brackets that best completes the sentence.

a) I met Mr. Suzuki last week, so he (can   should   would) remember me.

b) Dad is concerned the hurricane (might   must   should) get worse.

3. Replace the underlined word with the correct pronoun.

a) <u>Them</u> are leaving now. _____   **b)** Are they coming with <u>we?</u> _____

4. Does the adjective in the sentence tell *what kind* or *how many*?

These are useful tips to help set up the computer. _____

WEDNESDAY • Figures of Speech

1. Read the sentence. Identify the figure of speech.

  a) I'm so tired I could sleep standing up.　　(simile　hyperbole)

  b) Elephant is to huge as ant is to tiny.　　(metaphor　analogy)

2. Write an example of alliteration using the letter _A_.

_____

**3. a) Underline the animal or thing being personified in this sentence.
    Circle what it is doing to show that it is an example of personification.**

  The baby bird happily chatted with the other baby birds in the nest.

  b) Explain your thinking.

_____

THURSDAY • Vocabulary and Spelling

1. Write the contraction for each pair of words.

  a) can not _____ (don't can't)　**b)** will not _____ (won't wouldn't)

2. List two words that rhyme with the word _jump_.

_____

3. Circle the positive words. Underline the negative words.

lively　　shifty　　won't　　smiling　　never　　misbehave

4. Make three compound words using the words below.

fish　　book　　eye　　angel　　brow　　worm

_____　_____　_____

FRIDAY • Writing Prompt

Below is a quotation that offers some advice on how to live your life. Draw a picture.

1. a) Explain what you think the quotation below means.

"If you think someone can use a friend, then be one."

_____

_____

b) Do you think this is good advice? Explain your thinking.

_____

_____

_____

_____

☐ I checked for correct spelling.

☐ I checked for correct punctuation.

☐ I used interesting words.

☐ I organized my ideas in a way that makes sense.

☐ I used linking words to connect my ideas.

☐ Challenge: I used a figure of speech.

MONDAY • Sentences and Punctuation

1. **Write the correct punctuation mark at the end of each sentence. Name the sentence type.**

   a) Is it supposed to be sunny today _____   _____

   b) I love my pet so much _____   _____

2. **Add a comma between a street address, a town, and a province.**

   Harry lives at 15 Admiral Street Charlottetown Prince Edward Island.

3. **Circle the subject and verb that do not agree. Rewrite the sentence using the correct verb.**

   Mrs. Mavis draw some stick people on the board yesterday.

   _____

TUESDAY • Grammar and Usage

1. **Circle the main verb and underline the helping verb.**

   a) The forest fire is spreading quite quickly.

   b) I am reading an interesting book about dinosaurs.

2. **Rewrite the sentence to make the underlined nouns plural. Do not use the words *a* or *an* before a plural noun.**

   The <u>elf</u> ate a <u>sandwich</u> for lunch after making a <u>shelf</u> for a <u>toy</u>.

   _____

3. **Circle whether the adverbs in each sentence describe when, where, how, or how often.**

   a) I practise piano daily so I can play my best.   (when   where   how   how often)

   b) The man whistled happily as he walked home.   (when   where   how   how often)

WEDNESDAY • Figures of Speech

1. Read the sentence. Identify the figure of speech.

   a) Mom says potatoes are as cheap as dirt this week. (metaphor   simile)

   b) Jasmine's music told a dramatic tale of adventure. (oxymoron   personification)

2. Fill in the blank using hyperbole to make the sentence more exaggerated.

   I'm so tired that _____ .

3. Complete the simile.

   Waiting in a long line up is like _____ .

4. Use the oxymoron in a sentence to show its meaning.

   alone together

   _____

THURSDAY • Vocabulary and Spelling

1. Complete the sentence by writing *their*, *there*, or *they're*.

   _____ are twenty three students in _____ class.

2. Add a word that belongs to the group. math spelling science _____

3. Choose the best word to complete the sentence.

   Today was _____ than yesterday. (wet wetter wettest)

4. List a synonym for the word *tasty*. _____

5. List an antonym for the word *correct*. _____

6. Check the sentence for spelling. Rewrite the sentence.

   I choped some potatos for diner.

   _____

FRIDAY • Writing Prompt

A *recount* tells about events in the order that they happened.
Write a recount of an event that happened to you recently. Draw the event.

_____

_____

_____

_____

_____

_____

☐ I told the order of events with words like first, next, then, before, after, and finally.

☐ I ordered my ideas in a way that makes sense.

☐ I used "I" or "we" in my writing.

☐ I made sure to include details that answer who, what, where, when, and why.

☐ I checked for correct spelling and punctuation.

MONDAY • Sentences and Punctuation

1. Fill in the blank with the best conjunction.

We were cleaning up _____ we heard the doorbell ring.   (since   when)

2. Add commas to separate the items in a series.

The teacher gave us each some paper a pencil and an eraser for the test.

3. Add quotation marks and commas as necessary to the sentence.

Mom shouted Watch out for the big hole!

4. Rewrite the sentence to make the subject and verb agree.

Lots of snow fall all night. We has a snow day!

_____

TUESDAY • Grammar and Usage

1. Circle the correct verb.

a) Curtains or blinds (blocks   block) the sun from coming in.

b) Julian and Steve (pick   picks) strawberries in the field.

2. Write the correct pronoun to complete the sentence.

Can you help _____ with my homework?   (I   me)

3. Choose the correct preposition from the words in brackets.

I can't wait _____ the movie starts.   (until   before)

4. Does the adjective in the sentence tell *what kind* or *how many*?

There were several people waiting in line.   _____

WEDNESDAY • Figures of Speech

1. **Read the sentence. Identify the figure of speech.**

   a) His teeth chattered as he waited for the bus in the snow.   (metaphor onomatopoeia)

   b) That mouse is so tiny it could fit through a keyhole!   (hyperbole analogy)

2. **Write an example of alliteration using the letter *H*.**

   _____

3. **Use the oxymoron in a sentence to show its meaning.**

   open secret

   _____

4. **Underline the two things compared in the metaphor.**

   Hannah's bedroom is a zoo, with all her pets.

THURSDAY • Vocabulary and Spelling

1. **Circle the words that have the sound of *long o*.**
   Underline the words that have the sound of *short o*.

   bone   sock   frog   short   coat

2. **Fill in the blank with the correct word.**

   a) I can hardly _____ for the school trip!   (weight wait)

   b) The _____ of the boxes made them heavy to lift.   (weight wait)

3. **Write the contraction for each pair of words.**

   a) has not _____   (hasn't hadn't) b) must have _____   (mustn't must've)

4. **What is the best meaning of the underlined word?**

   Pablo became **sombre** when he heard the bad news.   (excited sad tired)

FRIDAY • Writing Prompt

A *procedure* is a set of numbered steps to follow to make or do something. Write a procedure for something that is easy to make or do.

Description

_____

_____

Materials or Ingredients

_____

_____

_____

Instructions

_____

_____

_____

_____

_____

_____

_____

☐ I have a description that tells what you will make or do.

☐ The information is organized under headings.

☐ I used sequencing words such as first, then, next and finally.

☐ I used action words to tell which actions to do.

☐ I checked for correct spelling and punctuation.

MONDAY • Sentences and Punctuation

1. Read the sentence. Circle the complete subject. Underline the complete predicate.

Louise and Ella hurried to their dance lesson.

2. Use a comma between the day and the year in a date.

My cousin's birthday is March 30 2002.

3. Fill in the blank with the correct conjunction.

Jean-Paul went straight home _____ he watched the movie.
(after   while)

4. Use a comma between a city or town and its province.

Millie and her family live in Victoria British Columbia.

TUESDAY • Grammar and Usage

1. Circle the main verb and underline the helping verb.

a) The left headlight on the car is flashing.

b) Our teacher has taught us about fractions.

2. Write the correct form of the verb in brackets to make the pronoun and verb agree.

She _____ homemade cookies each Saturday.   (make)

3. Choose the correct word to fill in the blank.

She hurt _____ when she slipped on sidewalk.   (her   herself)

Write *more* or *most* to complete each sentence correctly.

a) I get _____ excited for my birthday each day.

b) Summer is my _____ favourite season.

WEDNESDAY • Figures of Speech

1. Read the sentence. Identify the figure of speech.

a) Dad served us hot chili for dinner.　　(simile　oxymoron)

b) Dog is to bark as cat is to meow.　　(hyperbole　analogy)

2. Fill in the blank using hyperbole to make the sentence more exaggerated.

It will take me _____ to get ready.

**3. a) Underline the animal or thing being personified in this sentence.
Circle what it is doing to show that it is an example of personification.**

The last teddy bear on the shelf waited patiently for a child to take it home.

b) Explain your thinking.

_____

THURSDAY • Vocabulary and Spelling

1. Write the abbreviation for each word.

a) Suite _____　　**b)** tablespoon _____　　**c)** Junior _____

2. List two words that rhyme with the word *might*. _____　_____

3. Write the contraction for each pair of words.

a) do not _____　(don't　can't)

b) must not _____　(mustn't　must've)

4. Make three compound words using the words below.

crumbs　　dream　　place　　bread　　fire　　day

_____　_____　_____

5. How many syllables are there in the word *personification*? _____

FRIDAY • Writing Prompt

People ask for advice when they have a problem or would like an opinion about something. Give advice to someone about a specific situation.

_____
DATE

Dear _____ ,
GREETING

BODY

_____

_____

_____

_____

_____

_____

_____

_____

_____

_____

_____

Your friend, _____
CLOSING / SIGNATURE

☐ I checked for spelling and punctuation. ☐ I ordered my ideas in a way that makes sense.

MONDAY • Sentences and Punctuation

1. **Write the correct punctuation mark at the end of each sentence. Name the sentence type.**

   a) I don't believe it _____   _____

   b) I don't understand the question _____   _____

2. **Add quotation marks and all the correct punctuation to each sentence.**

   a) Cathy asked Do you have any brothers or sisters

   b) that cloud looks like a rabbit said May

3. **Rewrite the sentence using correct capitalization and punctuation.**

   does the salad have tomatoes lettuce and dressing

   _____

TUESDAY • Grammar and Usage

1. **Complete the sentence by writing the past tense of the verb in brackets.**

   a) Someone _____ (buy) the house that was for sale.

   b) Yesterday, I _____ (meet) my friends at the mall.

2. **Circle whether the adverb describes when, where, how, or how often.**

   a) My aunt works in that building there.   (when   where   how   how often)

   b) Katie never talks to strangers.   (when   where   how   how often)

3. **Is the word *swim* a noun or a verb? Circle the answer.**

   a) I am going for a swim in the lake.   (noun   verb)

   b) When did you learn how to swim?   (noun   verb)

4. **Circle the prepositions in the sentence.**   Go behind the last person in line.

Canadian Daily Language Skills, Grade 4   © Chalkboard Publishing Inc.

WEDNESDAY • Figures of Speech

1. Match each idiom to its correct meaning.

Idiom

around the clock

to run out of steam

Meaning

to feel tired

all the time

2. Read the sentence. Identify the figure of speech.

a) Peter picked up pretty pebbles in the park.　(hyperbole　alliteration)

b) The snaked hissed as it approached its prey.　(onomatopoeia　analogy)

3. Complete the simile.

a) The monster's feet were _____ .

b) The crowd was like _____ while listening to the concert.

THURSDAY • Vocabulary and Spelling

1. What does *cook* mean in this sentence? Underline the correct definition.

I am going to **cook** chili for dinner tonight.

(prepare food　　someone who prepares food)

2. Check the sentence for spelling. Rewrite the sentence.

Their were many childs at the berthday party.

_____

3. Write the contraction for each pair of words.

a) does not _____ (doesn't don't)　**b)** are not _____ (aren't won't)

4. List a synonym for the word *hard.* _____

5. List an antonym for the word *scared.* _____

FRIDAY • Writing Prompt

A *fact* is information that can be *proven* to be true. An *opinion* is a statement based on something a person *thinks* or *believes* to be true.

Fill in the table with two examples of facts and two examples of opinion.

Statement	Fact or Opinion	How do you know? Explain your thinking.

MONDAY • Sentences and Punctuation

1. What is missing in the sentence fragment below? Circle the answer.

the doll with the orange dress

(who or what is doing the action   the action   both are missing)

2. Rewrite the sentence fragment. Add what is missing to make a complete sentence.

_____

3. Fill in the blank with the correct conjunction.

Daniel likes to work on his invention _____ he comes home.
(as soon as   or)

4. Add quotation marks and all the correct punctuation to each sentence.

a) Can anyone tell us the answer asked Mr Lee   **b)** Spencer shouted I am over here

TUESDAY • Grammar and Usage

1. In each sentence, circle the correct possessive form of the noun in brackets.

a) This (sweater's   sweaters') sleeves are too long for me.

b) The daycare teacher put the (baby's   babies') toys while they were playing outside.

2. Circle the correct verb.

a) The boss and her employees (works   work) well together.

b) Heavy rain or snow (make   makes) driving more dangerous

3. Circle whether the adverb describes when, where, how, or how often.

a) Sometimes I eat popcorn for dessert.   (when   where   how   how often)

b) The kitten purred happily.   (when   where   how   how often)

WEDNESDAY • Figures of Speech

1. Read the sentence. Identify the figure of speech.

a) Orioles often eat oranges.   (alliteration   simile)

b) The hinges complained loudly as the door opened slowly.   (personification   analogy)

2. Fill in the blank using hyperbole to make the sentence more exaggerated.

Sheila waited _____ at the doctor's office.

3. Use each idiom in a sentence to show its correct meaning.

a) around the clock

_____

b) run out of steam

_____

THURSDAY • Vocabulary and Spelling

1. Write the contraction for each pair of words.

a) would not _____ (won't   wouldn't)

b) has not _____ (hasn't   hadn't)

2. Fill in the blank with the correct word.

a) Mrs. Patel and her _____ went to their appointment. (son   sun)

b) The _____ rises in the east and sets in the west. (son   sun)

3. Match a prefix and a base word to make three new words.

mis   re   un   fill   spell   done

_____   _____   _____

FRIDAY • Writing Prompt

A *proverb* is a saying that offers some advice on how to live your life.

[ ]

1. a) Explain what you think the proverb below means. Draw a picture.

"Gardens are not made by sitting in the shade."

_____

_____

b) Do you think this is good advice? Explain your thinking.

_____

_____

_____

_____

☐ I checked for correct spelling.   ☐ I organized my ideas in a way that makes sense.

☐ I checked for correct punctuation.   ☐ I used linking words to connect my ideas.

☐ I used interesting words.   ☐ Challenge: I used a figure of speech.

MONDAY • Sentences and Punctuation

1. Fill in the blank with the correct conjunction.

My friend likes to ski, _____ I prefer to snowboard.   (but   or)

2. Add commas to separate the items in a series.

Mr. Roy Ms. Patel and Mrs. Bull are teachers at our school.

3. Add quotation marks and all the correct punctuation to each sentence.

a) Dino groaned I still have to study for the test tomorrow

b) I aced the math test Tim exclaimed.

4. Use quotation marks around words that someone is speaking.

Who took the last cupcake? Vivian asked.

I did, Ziggy replied.

TUESDAY • Grammar and Usage

1. Circle the main verb and underline the helping verb.

a) The police officer will give the driver a ticket.

b) The tugboat will rescue the passengers from the sinking ship.

**2. Rewrite the sentence to make the underlined nouns plural.
Do not use the words *a* or *an* before a plural noun.**

The <u>wife</u> of the <u>chef</u> put a <u>loaf</u> of bread on the <u>shelf</u>.

_____

3. Choose the correct word to fill in the blank.

The hermit crab buried _____ in the sand.   (yourself   itself)

WEDNESDAY • Figures of Speech

1. Read the sentence. Identify the figure of speech.

a) You are the light of my life.   (metaphor   oxymoron)

b) The tiny hamster was as cute as a bug's ear.   (simile   metaphor)

2. Fill in the blank using hyperbole to make the sentence more exaggerated.

My aunt talks so loudly that she could _____ .

**3. a) Underline the animal or thing being personified in this sentence.
Circle what it is doing to show that it is an example of personification.**

The sneakers were exhausted after a long day of playing outside.

b) Explain your thinking.

_____

THURSDAY • Vocabulary and Spelling

1. Complete the sentence by writing _to, two,_ or _too_.

The trading cards cost _____ dollars.

2. Write the contraction for each pair of words.

a) can not _____ (couldn't can't)   **b)** will not _____ (won't wouldn't)

3. What is the best meaning of underlined word?

Jessica became **elated** when she heard she had won the prize.   (excited   sad   happy)

4. What is an antonym for _shout_? _____

5. What is a synonym for _old_? _____

6. List two words that rhyme with the word _crown._

_____

FRIDAY • Writing Prompt

A *recount* tells about events in the order that they happened.
Write a recount of an event that happened to a friend. Draw the event.

_____

_____

_____

_____

_____

_____

☐ I told the order of events with words like first, next, then, before, after, and finally.

☐ I ordered my ideas in a way that makes sense.

☐ I used "I" or "we" in my writing.

☐ I made sure to include details that answer who, what, where, when, and why.

☐ I checked for correct spelling and punctuation.

MONDAY • Sentences and Punctuation

1. **Read the sentence. Circle the complete subject. Underline the complete predicate.**

   The maple cookies tasted delicious.

2. **Add quotation marks and all the correct punctuation to each sentence.**

   a) Nathan shouted remember tomorrow is a holiday

   b) May I ride your new bike Sally asked

3. **Fill in the blank with the best conjunction.**

   a) My uncle has two pear trees, _____ he has a cherry tree.   (and   but)

   b) My brother is older than me, _____ I am taller.   (and   but)

TUESDAY • Grammar and Usage

1. **Complete the sentence by writing the past tense of the verb in brackets.**

   a) The librarian _____ (tell) the noisy children to be quiet.

   b) Gina _____ (leave) her backpack at her friend's house.

2. **Choose the correct preposition from the words in brackets.**

   The birds were flying high _____ the trees.   (above   under)

3. **Write the correct word below to complete each sentence.**

   that   which   who   whose

   a) The teacher chose someone _____ project was done.

   b) Our hotel, _____ is in downtown Toronto, has a great view of the lake.

WEDNESDAY • Figures of Speech

1. Draw a line to match the sentence to the correct figure of speech.

a) My grandfather says I'm the apple of his eye.   alliteration

b) Mom bought a package of jumbo shrimp.   analogy

c) The sun smiled down on us.   hyperbole

d) Sandy Smith sells sparkly stars to shoppers.   metaphor

e) He was as happy as a clam at high tide.   onomatopoeia

f) Ken's budgie chirps when it is fed.   oxymoron

g) It will take me two seconds to get ready to go.   personification

h) Plane is to fly as fish is to swim.   simile

2. What is an idiom that you have heard?

_____

THURSDAY • Vocabulary and Spelling

1. Add a word or phrase that belongs to the group.

New Brunswick   Manitoba   Prince Edward Island   _____

2. Write the contraction for each pair of words.

a) could not _____ (couldn't can't) **b)** would not _____ (won't wouldn't)

3. Match a prefix and a base word to make three new words.

im   re   in   shape   polite   complete

_____   _____   _____

4. Read the sentence for spelling mistakes. Rewrite the sentence.

Pleeze answer the door bell.

_____

FRIDAY • Writing Prompt

Write about something you are looking forward to. Explain why you are looking forward to it.

_____

_____

_____

_____

_____

_____

_____

☐ I checked for correct spelling.　　☐ I organized my ideas in a way that makes sense.

☐ I checked for correct punctuation.　☐ I used linking words to connect my ideas.

☐ I used interesting words.　　　　　☐ Challenge: I used a figure of speech.

Student Writing Tips

Sentence Starters

Sentence starters for **stating your opinion** in a piece of writing:

In my opinion…	I think…	The best thing about…
I feel…	I prefer…	The worst thing about…
I believe…	I know…	_____ is better than _____

Sentence starters to use **when trying to persuade someone** in a piece of writing:

Of course…	Clearly…	The fact is…
Without doubt…	Everyone knows that…	It is clear that…

Transition Words

Transition words or phrases to use **when providing reasons** in a piece of writing:

First of all…	Next…	Most importantly…
Secondly…	Another reason…	To begin with…

Transition words or phrases to use **when providing examples** in a piece of writing:

For example…	In fact…	In addition…
For instance…	In particular…	Another example…

Transition words or phrases to **show cause and effect** in a piece of writing:

For this reason…	As a result…	Consequently…
Because of [fact]…	Therefore…	Due to [reason]…

Transition words to use **when comparing or contrasting** in a piece of writing:

Similarly…	But…	Although…
Like…	However…	Even though…

Transition words or phrases to use **when showing a sequence** in a piece of writing:

First…	Next…	After that…
Second…	Eventually…	Lastly…

Transition words or phrases to use **when concluding** a piece of writing:

Finally…	Lastly…	All in all…
In conclusion…	To sum up…	As you can see…

 Canadian Daily Language Skills, Grade 4   © Chalkboard Publishing Inc.

Writing Planner

Ideas for My Paragraph

My Topic Sentence

What I Want to Say About the Topic

My Concluding Sentence

Adjectives for Writing

Category	Adjectives
Size	big, small, short, tall, fat, skinny, large, medium, slim, thin, slender, tiny, lean, scrawny, huge, gigantic, jumbo, plump, wee, wide, narrow
Shape	round, square, pointed, jagged, oval, chunky, curly, straight, curved, flat, twisted, heart-shaped, spiky, wavy, bent, tangled, messy
Colour	red, orange, yellow, green, blue, purple, pink, grey, white, black, brown, silver, gold
Age	young, old, new, baby, newborn
Sound	loud, quiet, long, short, musical, surprising, soft, noisy, muffled, whispering, growling, grumbling
Light and Brightness	dull, bright, dark, light, clear, flashy, flashing, dim, faint, glowing, flickering, twinkly, twinkling, shiny, shining
Smell	good, bad, strong, sweet, salty, spicy, stinky, sour, delicious, yummy, fresh, rotten, rotting
Feel and Texture	soft, hard, smooth, rough, silky, fluffy, fuzzy, furry, wet, dry, bumpy, lumpy, scratchy, sweaty, slippery, slimy, gritty, dirty, sticky, gummy, jiggly, wiggly, squishy, watery, liquid, solid, rock hard, damp, stiff, firm
Taste	delicious, bitter, sweet, salty, tasty, spicy, yummy, bland, sour, strong
Speed and Movement	quick, quickly, fast, slow, slowly, rapid, rapidly, brisk, briskly, swift, swiftly, instant, instantly, late
Temperature	hot, cold, icy, frosty, chilly, burning, boiling, steamy, sizzling, cool, warm, freezing, frozen, damp, humid, melting

How Am I Doing?

	Completing my work	Using my time wisely	Following directions	Keeping organized
Full speed ahead!	• My work is always complete and done with care. • I added extra details to my work.	• I always get my work done on time.	• I always follow directions.	• My materials are always neatly organized. • I am always prepared and ready to learn.
Keep going!	• My work is complete and done with care. • I added extra details to my work.	• I usually get my work done on time.	• I usually follow directions without reminders.	• I usually can find my materials. • I am usually prepared and ready to learn.
Slow down!	• My work is complete. • I need to check my work.	• I sometimes get my work done on time.	• I sometimes need reminders to follow directions.	• I sometimes need time to find my materials. • I am sometimes prepared and ready to learn.
Stop!	• My work is not complete. • I need to check my work.	• I rarely get my work done on time.	• I need reminders to follow directions.	• I need to organize my materials. • I am rarely prepared and ready to learn.

_____'s *Completion Chart*

Week	Monday	Tuesday	Wednesday	Thursday	Friday
1					
2					
3					
4					
5					
6					
7					
8					
9					
10					
11					
12					
13					
14					
15					
16					
17					
18					
19					
20					
21					
22					
23					
24					
25					
26					
27					
28					
29					
30					
31					
32					
33					
34					
35					

Achievement Award

Fantastic Work!

Canadian Daily Language Skills, Grade 4

Answers to Exercises

WEEK 1, pp. 3–5

Monday **1. Complete Sentence** I collected seashells on the beach. **Sentence Fragment** Seashells on the beach.
2. a) The soccer game b) The neighbourhood children
3. a) is on Sunday afternoon. b) played baseball in the field.
Tuesday **1. Nouns** tree, sky, song, pape,r beach, mall, baseball, mountain, house, **Verbs** drive, si,t sing, play, run, watch, feel, dance, **Adjectives** happy, wonderful, kind, clear, large, fast, tiny **2.** Answers will vary. Ensure the proper nouns are capitalized.
Wednesday **1.** Literal; Figurative **2.** Casey cut the cloth to create a cute carryall. **3.** a) drink
Thursday **1.** a) read b) important **2.** a) shut b) happiness
3. a) none b) worst
Friday Answers will vary. Ensure the child has covered the items in, and marked off, the checklist at the bottom of the exercise.

WEEK 2, pp. 6–8

Monday **1.** a) exclamation mark or period b) question mark c) period d) period **2. Complete Subject** Andrew and Pria **Complete Predicate** went to the soccer championship game.
Tuesday **1.** a) a b) an c) an d) a **2. Common Nouns** hike birds **Proper Nouns** Sunday, Mr. Turnbull, Milton Park
3. a) **Adjective** black **Noun** spider b) **Adjective** favourite **Noun** toy **4.** a) howled b) arrested
Wednesday **1.** Answers will vary. Ensure the phrase is an exaggeration. **2.** is scared of everything
Thursday **1.** a) Blue b) blew **2.** a) town b) while c) stick
3. put on clothes
Friday Answers will vary. Ensure the child has covered the items in, and marked off, the checklist at the bottom of the exercise.

WEEK 3, pp. 9–11

Monday **1.** or **2.** The city of Ottawa is the capital of Canada. **3.** a) the action b) Answers will vary. Ensure the sentence includes a verb that agrees with the subject.
Tuesday **1.** a) boxes b) glasses c) dolls d) flies e) books f) wishes g) beaches h) foxes **2.** a) can b) might
3. Adjective cold **Noun** water **Adjective** fresh **Noun** vegetables
Wednesday **1.** My new baby sister is as cute as a button.
2. Answers will vary. Sample answers: a mile wide; a metre wide; a yard wide **3.** eat
Thursday **1.** a) refuse b) basement **2.** power, force, strength

114

3. a) flour b) flower **4.** a) Sat. b) Tues. c) Fri.
Friday Answers will vary. Ensure the child has covered the items in, and marked off, the checklist at the bottom of the exercise.

WEEK 4, pp. 12–14

Monday **1.** a) RO b) ✔ **2.** a) question mark; question b) period; command **3.** My brother's birthday is June 15, 2002.
Tuesday **1.** a) they, them b) she, her c) we, us **2.** under
3. a) meant b) lay
Wednesday **1.** a) Billy the bulldog bounces the brown ball. b) Ellie the elephant eats everything. **2.** feels sad
3. Answers will vary. Ensure the sentences include **as** or **like**.
Thursday **1.** a) I've b) you've **2.** too, to **3.** sun
4. friendly
Friday Answers will vary. Ensure the child has covered the items in, and marked off, the checklist at the bottom of the exercise.

WEEK 5, pp. 15–17

Monday **1.** a) My favourite colours are blue, red, and purple. b) For lunch we had sandwiches, carrot sticks, and chocolate milk. c) Robins, cardinals, and blue jays are types of birds. **2.** a) and b) but
Tuesday **1.** a) **Adverb** today **Verb** Come b) **Adverb** Later **Verb** are going c) **Adverb** Tonight **Verb** have d) **Adverb** tomorrow **Verb** am going shopping **2.** a) must b) will
3. a) is b) take
Wednesday **1.** a) yes b) yes **2.** fire **3.** a) ✔ **4.** Answers will vary. Sample answer: a clam
Thursday **1.** best **2.** sleep, cake, are **3.** fetch, get, retrieve **4.** a) impress b) speech
Friday Answers will vary. Ensure the first letters spell the child's name when read vertically.

WEEK 6, pp. 18–20

Monday **1.** a) "I hope we have good weather on the weekend," Dad said. b) "I wonder if she noticed that we came in late," whispered Nicole **2.** Is the train on time?
Tuesday **1.** a) the animals' habitat b) the shark's teeth c) the five geese's feathers d) the spider's web
Wednesday **1.** Answers will vary. Ensure the choice of words reflects an understanding of alliteration. **2.** short
3. My little brother never stops talking! ✔ **4.** cost a lot of money

Thursday **1.** a) appear b) correct **2.** mistake **3.** a) lose b) never **4.** a) afternoon b) nothing **5.** a) pinch something b) pull hair

Friday Answers will vary. Ensure the child has covered the items in, and marked off, the checklist at the bottom of the exercise.

WEEK 7, pp. 21–23

Monday **1.** I have a pet fish, hamster, and cat. **2.** "I think the test is on Thursday," Julie said. **3.** Mr. and Mrs. Sully are going to Mario's Pizzeria for dinner. **4.** Spot is chasing a cat. Spot won't stop.

Tuesday **1.** a) loaves b) wolves c) scarves **2.** a) chefs b) cliffs c) roofs **3.** sketches **4.** a) I b) me

Wednesday **1.** a) oink, munches b) moo c) barked **2.** pretty ugly; big baby

Thursday **1.** un, ing, fold; dis, ed, count **2.** three **3.** Answers will vary. Sample answers: pail, whale, dale, kale, shale, fail, veil, rail, sale, they'll **4.** **Positive** fluffy, sparkling, cheerful **Negative** nonsense, itchy, grouchy, sore

Friday Answers will vary. Ensure the child has covered the items in, and marked off, the checklist at the bottom of the exercise.

WEEK 8, pp. 24–26

Monday **1.** a) "Would you like to look through the telescope?" the scientist asked. b) "We won the championship!" shouted Mike. **2.** **Complete Subject** The tall tree **Complete Predicate** swayed dangerously in the strong wind.

Tuesday **1.** a) must b) can **2.** a) caught b) shook **3.** a) **Adverb** slowly **Verb** walked b) **Adverb** quickly **Verb** got dressed **4.** a) him b) her

Wednesday **1.** a) hope, walked b) leaves, danced **2.** The cat's eyes gleamed like diamonds. ✔

Thursday **1.** a) they'll b) we'd **2.** a) bored b) board **3.** We are going shopping on Saturday.

Friday Answers will vary. Ensure the child has covered the items in, and marked off, the checklist at the bottom of the exercise.

WEEK 9, pp. 27–29

Monday **1.** who or what is doing the action **2.** Answers will vary. Ensure the complete sentence has a subject and verb that agree. **3.** I play on a soccer team with Wyatt, Andrew, and Felix. **4.** a) "Who took the last cupcake?" Carlos asked. b) "This is the best pizza!" exclaimed Abbie and Jacob.

Tuesday **1.** a) the teachers' b) the fairies' c) the pig's **2.** a) entered b) picks **3.** **Adjective** old **Noun** car **Adjective**

winding **Noun** road **Adjective** early **Noun** morning

Wednesday **1.** Answers will vary for a) and b). Sample answers: a) parrot, bat, eagle b) lion, waterfall, thunder **2.** a) cold sweat b) only choice **3.** Answers will vary. Ensure the sentence reflects an understanding of oxymorons. **4.** light, conquered

Thursday **1.** a) Sun. b) Wed. c) Mon. **2.** a) straight b) safe **3.** edge, boundary, margin perimeter **4.** unlocked **5.** to, too

Friday Answers will vary. Ensure the child has covered the items in, and marked off, the checklist at the bottom of the exercise.

WEEK 10, pp. 30–32

Monday **1.** a) ✔ b) RO **2.** I am starving! **or** I am starving. **3.** The storekeeper announced, "We are closing in half an hour."

Tuesday **1.** a) walk b) helps **2.** a) knives b) lives c) wives **3.** a) the b) a, an **4.** better

Wednesday **1.** **Idiom** slipped my mind **Meaning** forgot **Idiom** time flies **Meaning** goes by fast **Idiom** be all ears **Meaning** listen **Idiom** break a leg **Meaning** good luck **2.** rumble boom clash glug cluck **3.** Answers will vary for a) and b). Ensure the sentence includes **as** or **like**.

Thursday **1.** **Long a** aim fame day baby **Short a** cat flag map **2.** a) doesn't b) shouldn't **3.** a) (H b) A c) S **4.** causing little effort or trouble

Friday Answers will vary. Ensure the child has covered the items in, and marked off, the checklist at the bottom of the exercise.

WEEK 11, pp. 33–35

Monday **1.** a) Leanne exclaimed, "That was an amazing presentation!" b) Ms. Finch said, "Please open your books to page 35." **2.** a) period; statement b) exclamation mark; exclamation **3.** There are swings, monkey bars, and trapeze rings at the playground.

Tuesday **1.** a) interviewed b) records **2.** a) park b) walk **3.** a) here b) away **4.** me

Wednesday **1.** Answers will vary for a) and b). Sample answers: a) I meant to buy a notebook but it completely slipped my mind. b) Time flies when you're at the ballgame! **or** Don't you find time flies when you're on holiday? **2.** a) awfully good b) silent scream **3.** jalopy, wheezed

Thursday **1.** in, ly, correct; re, ing, fresh **2.** a) I'd b) you've c) they'll **3.** a) sum b) some

Friday Answers will vary. Ensure the poems follow the format of two syllables, four syllables, six syllables, eight syllables, two syllables.

WEEK 12, pp. 36–38

Monday   1. Complete Subject Our whole family
Complete Predicate went on a vacation to Banff National
Park.   **2.** Put the knives, spoons, and forks in the drawer. **or**
Put the knives, spoons, and forks in the drawer!
3. a) Yes, I look forward to attending the party. b) No, I have
not seen that movie.   **4.** Dad warned, "Do not go near the
construction site!"
Tuesday   1. might   **2. Common Nouns** chocolates,
teacher **Proper Nouns** Valentine's Day, Mrs. Alderson
3. We   **4.** tastiest
Wednesday   1. Answers will vary for a) and b). Sample
answers: a) Tell me your secret—I'm all ears. b) Your play
opens tonight, so, break a leg!   **2.** tall   **3.** Answers will
vary. Ensure the sentences reflect an understanding of
hyperbole.
Thursday   1. a) remember b) follower   **2.** rush, scurry,
dash   **3.** their, they're   **4.** words that have magic powers
Friday   Answers will vary. Ensure the child has covered
the items in, and marked off, the checklist at the bottom of
the exercise.

WEEK 13, pp. 39–41
Monday   1. a) "Max, can you come over on Saturday?"
Kyle asked. b) Max answered, "I sure can, Kyle."   **2.** both
are missing
Tuesday   1. a) my friend's b) the deer's c) the bunnies'
2. a) illustrate b) performs   **3.** a) fishes b) people c) glasses
Wednesday   1. Idiom crack a book **Meaning** open a book
and read **Idiom** in the bag **Meaning** be certain   **2.** a) yes
b) yes c) no d) yes
Thursday   1. mis, ed, guide; re, ing, form   **2.** a) paws
b) pause   **3.** a) k b) c) e   **4.** four
Friday   Answers will vary. Ensure the child has covered
the items in, and marked off, the checklist at the bottom of
the exercise.

WEEK 14, pp. 42–44

Monday   1. a) or b) so   **2.** We had salad, meatloaf, and
potatoes for dinner.   **3.** a) Mrs. Mendez said, "Holly, are you
able to babysit this afternoon?" b) Holly responded, "No, I
am sorry."   **4.** Answers will vary. The sentence may end with
either a period or an exclamation mark.
Tuesday   1. a) spent b) read   **2.** a) would b) May
3. a) always b) twice
Wednesday   1. Answers will vary for a) and b). Sample
answers: a) I don't think Buddy's cracked a book in two
years. b) I'm going to win the contest—it's in the bag.
2. a) endless hour b) honest thief   **3.** Answers will vary.
Ensure the sentence includes a repetition of sounds.
Thursday   1. a) S b) H c) A   **2.** a) st. b) June
c) dr. **or** Dr.

3. a) they'd b) we've   **4.** carried   **5.** a) complain about this
b) slam the door
Friday   Answers will vary. The child should have reasons
for his or her argument.

WEEK 15, pp. 45–47

Monday   1. a) RO b) RO   **2.** a) question mark; question
b) period or exclamation mark; command   **3.** The parent
council includes parents, teachers, and the principal
Tuesday   1. Main Verb watching **Helping Verb** were
2. a) myself b) herself
Wednesday   1. a) highway, parking lot b) Answers will vary.
Sample answer: Traffic was so bad on Friday the highway
was a parking lot.   **2.** a) yes b) no c) yes d) yes
3. strawberry = **red** as blueberry = **blue**
Thursday   1. a) synonyms b) antonyms c) antonyms
d) synonyms   **2.** unexpected, recovering   **3.** drop
Friday   Answers will vary. Ensure the child has covered
the items in, and marked off, the checklist at the bottom of
the exercise.

WEEK 16, pp. 48-50

Monday   1. Complete Subject The rude student
Complete Predicate interrupted the teacher.   **2.** a) RO
b) ✔   **3.** Answers will vary. Ensure the sentence ends
with a question mark.   **4.** a) Samantha yelled, "Simon,
you cheated!" b) "Why do I always have to take out the
garbage?" complained Kim.
Tuesday   1. a) fishermen's b) branch's   **2.** a) surveyed
b) suggests   **3.** wild, before; soft, before
Wednesday   1. Answers will vary for a) and b). Sample
answers: a) thud, plop b) burp, belch   **2.** found missing;
mud bath; oven fried   **3.** Answers will vary. Ensure the
sentence includes **as** or **like**.   **4.** lunch, did not agree
Thursday   1. a) horse b) hoarse   **2.** boots   **3.** a) pre b) re
4. toothbrush, starfish, haircut
Friday   Answers will vary. Ensure the child follows the
format of a Diamond poem using nouns, verbs, and
adjectives.

WEEK 17, pp. 51-53

Monday   1. when   **2.** a) Yes, I had a visit with my aunt
and uncle. b) No, you cannot go to the store.   **3.** Answers
will vary. Ensure the subject and verb agree.   **4.** Yes, I had
heard that Dr. Gotti is moving to Brandon, Manitoba, in
September.
Tuesday   1. a) kept b) became   **2.** a) should b) could
3. a) echoes b) potatoes c) heroes
Wednesday   1. Idiom to get cold feet **Meaning** to be

nervous **Idiom** to get up on the wrong side of the bed **Meaning** to be cranky 2. Answers will vary. Sample answers: a) a pig b) a clock 3. a) disgustingly delicious b) Answers will vary. Sample answer: The cake was really (**or** almost too) rich and tasty.

Thursday 1. to, too 2. a) she'd b) he'll 3. geese
4. Answers will vary. Ensure the word has two syllables.
5. cm, km, ml **or** mL

Friday Answers will vary. Ensure the child has covered the items in, and marked off, the checklist at the bottom of the exercise.

WEEK 18 pp54-56

Monday 1. both are missing 2. Answers will vary. Ensure the sentence has a subject and verb that agree. 3. My favourite fruits are bananas, pineapples, and oranges.
4. Halifax is the capital of Nova Scotia.

Tuesday 1. **Main Verb** told **Helping Verb** has 2.
Common Nouns office, building **Proper Nouns** Dr. Garret; Oxford Street; London; Ontario. 3. us

Wednesday 1. Answers will vary for a) and b). Sample answers: a) I'm starting to get cold feet about competing in the race tomorrow. b) Boy, did the coach get up on the wrong side of the bed this morning! 2. nose 3. Answers will vary. Ensure the sentence includes a repetition of sounds.

Thursday 1. a) race, soft c; cat, hard c b) large, soft g; gate, hard g 2. uneventful 3. prize 4. In June, Dr. Sotto will travel to Winnipeg.

Friday Answers will vary. Ensure the child has covered the items in, and marked off, the checklist at the bottom of the exercise.

WEEK 19, pp. 57–59

Monday 1. until 2. Answers will vary. Ensure the predicate includes a verb that agrees with the subject.
3. Do not tell me what to do. **or** Do not tell me what to do!
4. a) Jacques yelled, "Be careful!" b) "Where can I find a pencil sharpener?" asked Dmitri.

Tuesday 1. meet 2. a) verb b) noun 3. hike
4. **Adjectives** warm, many, school **Nouns** day, children, playground

Wednesday 1. a) least favourite b) Answers will vary. Sample answer: We're having a test tomorrow in my least favourite class: health! 2. a) books, keys b) Answers will vary. Sample answer: Reading helps you imagine different things. 3. Answers will vary. Ensure the sentence includes a repetition of sounds.

Thursday 1. a) Feb. b) Mr. c) Ont. 2. a) Danger b) sick
3. a) present b) succeed

Friday Answers will vary. Ensure the child has covered the items in, and marked off, the checklist at the bottom of the exercise.

WEEK 20, pp. 60–62

Monday 1. **Complete Subject** Ben's older brother **Complete Predicate** plays on the basketball team.
2. a) exclamation mark **or** period; exclamation **or** statement b) exclamation mark **or** period; command 3. Answers will vary. Ensure the sentence uses correct capitalization and punctuation. 4. I need a pencil, an eraser, paper, and a place to do homework.

Tuesday 1. a) book's b) boxers' 2. a) interrupted
b) growls 3. you 4. on

Wednesday 1. **Idiom** a long shot **Meaning** a small possibility **Idiom** to be sick as a dog **Meaning** to feel really sick 2. a) school, sad b) Answers will vary. Sample answer: People, not buildings, experience sadness. 3. Answers will vary. Ensure the sentence reflects an understanding of hyperbole.

Thursday 1. **Long u** huge, few, tube, cute **Short u** bug, sun 2. Answers will vary. The child should choose one of the following: Jan. Feb. Mar. Apr. May June July Aug. Sept. Oct. Nov. Dec. 3. a) I'm, I am b) They're, they are 4. Ravi was thrilled about getting a puppy.

Friday Answers will vary. Ensure the child has covered the items in, and marked off, the checklist at the bottom of the exercise.

WEEK 21, pp. 63–65

Monday 1. before 2. The recipe calls for milk, flour, butter, and eggs. 3. Janelle asked, "What time do we need to leave?" 4. This is the worst meal I have ever eaten!

Tuesday 1. a) rose b) chose 2. I 3. Answers will vary. Ensure the sentence uses an adverb that tells **where** an action happens, such as up, down, there, nearby.
4. smaller

Wednesday 1. Answers will vary for a) and b). Sample answers: a) I hoped to win $50, but I knew it was a long shot. b) Tia couldn't come to the party because she's sick as a dog. 2. a) yes, b) no 3. Answers will vary. Ensure the sentence includes **as** or **like**.

Thursday 1. their 2. a) she'll b) he'd 3. mice 4. a) steel b) steal 5. Answers will vary. Ensure the word has four syllables.

Friday Answers will vary. Ensure the child has covered the items in, and marked off, the checklist at the bottom of the exercise.

Monday **1.** a) RO b) ✔ **2.** a) "I can't wait for the field trip!" exclaimed Jaffir. b) "Tao, we are so excited to come and see you in the school play," said Mom and Dad. **3.** Answers will vary. Ensure the subject includes a noun or pronoun that agrees with the verb.
Tuesday **1.** a) **Main Verb** going **Helping Verb** am b) **Main Verb** running **Helping Verb** was **2. Common Nouns** cousin, shoes, sandals **Proper Nouns** Mary, Fancy Footwear, Boxing Day **3.** Answers will vary. Ensure the sentence uses an adverb that tells **when** an action happens such as yesterday, tomorrow, weekly.
Wednesday **1.** a) sun, beat down b) Answers will vary. Sample answer: Only people, not the sun, are able to beat down on anything. **2.** a) splash b) squirted **3.** voice, music
Thursday **1.** a celebration meal **2.** a) couldn't b) wouldn't **3.** a) mis b) un **4.** Answers will vary. Sample answers: school, fool, rule, cool, ghoul, spool
Friday Answers will vary. Ensure the child has covered the items in, and marked off, the checklist at the bottom of the exercise.

Monday **1.** as soon as **2.** who or what is doing the action **3.** Answers will vary. Ensure the complete sentence has a subject and a verb that agree. **4.** The girl opened the book. She read it in the cozy chair.
Tuesday **1.** a) Could b) would **2.** a) drives b) rush **3.** The children watched videos and played games.
Wednesday **1.** a) clearly confused b) Answers will vary. Sample answer: It was obvious he was mixed up. **2.** green **3.** a) laughter, medicine b) Answers will vary. Sample answer: When you're feeling low, all you need is a laugh to cheer you up.
Thursday **1.** a) h b) g, h c) h, t, e **2.** a) we'll b) you'll **3.** a) synonyms b) antonyms c) synonyms d) antonyms **4.** five
Friday Answers will vary. Ensure the child has covered the items in, and marked off, the checklist at the bottom of the exercise.

Monday **1. Complete Subject** The laughing children **Complete Predicate** tracked mud as they came inside the house. **2.** a) period; statement b) question mark; question **3.** Please pick up eggs, bread, and cheese at the grocery store. **4.** called
Tuesday **1.** a) built b) felt **2.** We went to the library. **3.** for **4.** most

Wednesday **1.** Answers will vary. Ensure the sentence includes a repetition of sounds. **2.** a) Answers will vary. Sample answer: a snail's trail. b) Answers will vary. **3.** a) temper, volcano b) Answers will vary. Sample answer: Bruno looked very calm, but his temper was a volcano.
Thursday **1.** a) Jr. b) Ave. c) Blvd. **2.** a) mistake b) rush **3.** a) whole b) hole
Friday Answers will vary. Ensure the child has covered the items in, and marked off, the checklist at the bottom of the exercise

Monday **1.** a) Yes, I would like another helping of pie. b) No, I am leaving in the morning. **2.** while **3.** "Alex, would you like to share your story with the class?" Mrs. Turnbull asked. **4.** Is it true that Valentine's Day is Morgan's favourite holiday?
Tuesday **1.** a) **Main Verb** swimming **Helping Verb** are b) **Main Verb** dripping **Helping Verb** was **2. Common Nouns** burgers, fries, milkshakes **Proper Nouns** Harry's Burger Bar; Clearview Mall **3.** I **4.** what kind
Wednesday **1.** a) hockey puck; flew b) Answers will vary. Sample answer: Inanimate objects are not able to fly. **2.** Answers will vary for a) and b). Ensure the sentences reflect an understanding of hyperbole.
Thursday **1. Long i** shine, night, cry **Short i** fit, milk **2.** Answers will vary. Sample answers: quick, speedy, rapid, swift **3.** Answers will vary. Sample answers: loud, noisy, deafening, ear-splitting **4.** four **5.** Answers will vary. Sample answer: We had to show we were old enough to get into the show.
Friday Answers will vary. Ensure the child has covered the items in, and marked off, the checklist at the bottom of the exercise.

Monday **1.** a) "Monster Reunion is the funniest movie ever!" exclaimed Eva. b) "Watch for that car!" yelled Tommy. **2.** because **3.** Eat your vegetables now! **or** Eat your vegetables now.
Tuesday **1.** a) teams' b) markers' **2.** a) locks b) fall **3.** a) He b) We **4.** Answers will vary. Ensure the adjectives are appropriate to the nouns they describe.
Wednesday **1. Idiom** zip your lip **Meaning** be very quiet **Idiom** over the moon **Meaning** very happy **2.** Answers will vary. Ensure the sentence includes a repetition of sounds. **3.** a) my grandma's dog; stubborn mule b) tears; a river **4.** Answers will vary. Sample answer: When the principal comes in, just act naturally.

Thursday 1. two, to 2. a) isn't b) it's 3. a) rip b) slap c) ran off 4. Their house is on the same street as my cousin's.
Friday Answers will vary. Ensure the child has covered the items in, and marked off, the checklist at the bottom of the exercise.

WEEK 27, pp. 81–83

Monday 1. **Complete Subject** My baby brother **Complete Predicate** broke my remote-controlled car.
2. a) exclamation mark; exclamation b) period; statement
3. I need sunglasses, sunscreen, and a sun hat for the beach. 4. Mr. Tanaka gives out homework every Friday afternoon.
Tuesday 1. a) **Main Verb** discussed **Helping Verb** have b) **Main Verb** erupt **Helping Verb** will 2. travel **or** will travel 3. A, a, an 4. Answers will vary. Ensure the sentence uses an adverb that tells **how often** an action happens, such as always, never, frequently.
Wednesday 1. a) metaphor b) hyperbole 2. Answers will vary for a) and b). Sample answers: a) If they ask you where you were this afternoon, just zip your lip! b) She was over the moon because she ran the marathon in record time. 3. Answers will vary. Ensure the sentence includes **as** or **like**.
Thursday 1. terrible or awful 2. a) worn b) warn 3. circulate, circus
Friday Answers will vary. Ensure the child has covered the items in, and marked off, the checklist at the bottom of the exercise.

WEEK 28, pp. 84–86

Monday 1. a) "Have you seen my bike?" Debbie asked John. b) "Fetch the stick!" Mom said to our dog. 2. since 3. who or what is doing the action 4. Answers will vary. Ensure the complete sentence has a subject and a verb that agree.
Tuesday 1. a) spoke b) paid 2. a) should b) might 3. a) They b) us 4. what kind
Wednesday 1. a) hyperbole b) analogy 2. Answers will vary. Ensure the sentence includes a repetition of sounds. 3. a) bird, chatted b) Answers will vary. Sample answer: People, not birds, are able to chat.
Thursday 1. a) can't b) won't 2. Answers will vary. Sample answers: bump, clump, dump, lump, hump, pump 3. **Positive** lively, smiling **Negative** shifty, won't, never, misbehave 4. angelfish, bookworm, eyebrow
Friday Answers will vary. Ensure the child has covered the items in, and marked off, the checklist at the bottom of the exercise.

WEEK 29, pp. 87–89

Monday 1. a) question mark; question b) exclamation mark; exclamation 2. Harry lives at 15 Admiral Street, Charlottetown, Prince Edward Island. 3. Mrs. Mavis, draw; Mrs. Mavis drew some stick people on the board yesterday.
Tuesday 1. **Main Verb** spreading **Helping Verb** is **Main Verb** reading **Helping Verb** am 2. The elves ate sandwiches for lunch after making shelves for toys. 3. a) daily, when; best, how b) happily, how; home, where
Wednesday 1. a) simile b) personification 2. Answers will vary. Ensure the sentence reflects an understanding of hyperbole. 3. Answers will vary. Ensure the sentence includes **as** or **like**. 4. Answers will vary. Sample answer: Since they needed to talk, we left the mother and her child alone together.
Thursday 1. There, their 2. Answers will vary. Sample answers: geography, social studies, health 3. wetter 4. Answers will vary. Sample answers: delicious, yummy, scrumptious 5. Answers will vary. Sample answers: wrong, mistaken, incorrect, erroneous
Friday Answers will vary. Ensure the child has covered the items in, and marked off, the checklist at the bottom of the exercise.

WEEK 30, pp. 90–92

Monday 1. when 2. The teacher gave us each some paper, a pencil, and an eraser for the test. 3. Mom shouted, "Watch out for the big hole!" 4. Lots of snow fell all night. We have a snow day!
Tuesday 1. a) block b) pick 2. me 3. until 4. how many
Wednesday 1. a) onomatopoeia b) hyperbole 2. Answers will vary. Ensure the sentence includes a repetition of sounds. 3. Answers will vary. Sample answer: It's an open secret that Paulo has a crush on Janelle. 4. bedroom, zoo
Thursday 1. **Long o** bone, short, coat **Short o** sock, frog 2. a) wait b) weight 3. a) hasn't b) must've 4. sad
Friday Answers will vary. Ensure the child has covered the items in, and marked off, the checklist at the bottom of the exercise.

WEEK 31, pp. 93–95

Monday 1. **Complete Subject** Louise and Ella **Complete Predicate** hurried to their dance lesson. 2. My cousin's birthday is March 30, 2002. 3. after 4. Millie and her family live in Victoria, British Columbia.
Tuesday 1. a) **Main Verb** flashing **Helping Verb** is b) **Main Verb** taught **Helping Verb** has 2. makes 3. herself 4. a) more b) most

Wednesday   **1.** a) oxymoron b) analogy   **2.** Answers will vary. Ensure the sentence reflects an understanding of hyperbole.   **3.** a) teddy bear, waited b) Answers will vary. Sample answer: People, not stuffed animals, can wait patiently.

Thursday   **1.** a) Ste. b) tbsp **or** Tbsp. c) Sr.   **2.** Answers will vary. Sample answers: bite, height, cite, quite, write   **3.** a) don't b) mustn't   **4.** breadcrumbs, daydream, fireplace   **5.** six

Friday   Answers will vary. Ensure the child has covered the items in, and marked off, the checklist at the bottom of the exercise.

WEEK 32, pp. 96–98

Monday   **1.** a) exclamation mark **or** period; exclamation **or** statement b) period; statement   **2.** a) Cathy asked, "Do you have any brothers or sisters?" b) "That cloud looks like a rabbit," said May. **or** "That cloud looks like a rabbit!" said May.   **3.** Does the salad have tomatoes, lettuce, and dressing?

Tuesday   **1.** a) bought b) met   **2.** a) where b) how often   **3.** a) noun b) verb   **4.** behind, in

Wednesday   **1. Idiom** around the clock **Meaning** all the time **Idiom** to run out of steam **Meaning** to feel tired   **2.** a) alliteration b) onomatopoeia   **3.** Answers will vary for a) and b). Ensure the sentences include **as** or **like**.

Thursday   **1.** prepare food   **2.** There were many children at the birthday party.   **3.** a) doesn't b) aren't   **4.** Answers will vary. Sample answers: difficult, challenging, tough, solid   **5.** Answers will vary. Sample answers: unafraid, fearless, bold, brave, daring

Friday   Answers will vary. The child should have reasons for his or her argument.

WEEK 33, pp. 99–101

Monday   **1.** the action   **2.** Answers will vary. Ensure the complete sentence has a subject and a verb that agree.   **3.** as soon as   **4.** a) "Can anyone tell us the answer?" asked Mr. Lee. b) Spencer shouted, "I am over here!"

Tuesday   **1.** a) sweater's b) babies'   **2.** a) work b) makes   **3.** a) how often b) how

Wednesday   **1.** a) alliteration b) personification   **2.** Answers will vary. Ensure the sentence reflects an understanding of hyperbole.   **3.** Answers will vary for a) and b). Sample answers: a) Between lacrosse practice and school, she was going around the clock. b) Sal couldn't finish the race; he just ran out of steam.

Thursday   **1.** a) wouldn't b) hasn't   **2.** a) son b) sun   **3.** misspell, refill, undone

Friday   Answers will vary. Ensure the child has covered the items in, and marked off, the checklist at the bottom of the exercise.

WEEK 34, pp. 102–104

Monday   **1.** but   **2.** Mr. Roy, Ms. Patel, and Mrs. Bull are teachers at our school.   **3.** a) Dino groaned, "I still have to study for the test tomorrow." b) "I aced the math test!" Tim exclaimed.   **4.** "Who took the last cupcake?" Vivian asked. "I did," Ziggy replied.

Tuesday   **1.** a) **Main Verb** give **Helping Verb** will b) **Main Verb** rescue **Helping Verb** will   **2.** The wives of the chefs put loaves of bread on the shelves.   **3.** itself

Wednesday   **1.** a) metaphor b) simile   **2.** Answers will vary. Ensure the sentence reflects an understanding of hyperbole.   **3.** a) sneakers, exhausted; b) Answers will vary. Sample answer: People, not shoes, feel exhausted.

Thursday   **1.** two   **2.** a) can't b) won't   **3.** happy   **4.** Answers will vary. Sample answers: whisper, murmur, breathe, mumble   **5.** Answers will vary. Sample answers: elderly, ancient, grizzled, hoary   **6.** Answers will vary. Sample answers: down, frown, clown, noun, town

Friday   Answers will vary. Ensure the child has covered the items in, and marked off, the checklist at the bottom of the exercise.

WEEK 35, pp. 105–107

Monday   **1. Complete Subject** The maple cookies **Complete Predicate** tasted delicious.   **2.** a) Nathan shouted, "Remember, tomorrow is a holiday!" b) "May I ride your new bike?" Sally asked.   **3.** a) and b) but

Tuesday   **1.** a) told b) left   **2.** above   **3.** a) The teacher chose someone whose project was done. b) Our hotel, which is in downtown Toronto, has a great view of the lake.

Wednesday   **1.** a) metaphor b) oxymoron c) personification d) alliteration e) simile f) onomatopoeia g) hyperbole h) analogy   **2.** Answers will vary.

Thursday   **1.** Answers will vary. The child should choose one of the following: British Columbia, Alberta, Saskatchewan, Ontario, Quebec, Nova Scotia, Newfoundland, Nunavut, Whitehorse, Yukon   **2.** a) couldn't b) wouldn't   **3.** reshape, impolite, incomplete   **4.** Please answer the doorbell.

Friday   Answers will vary. Ensure the child has covered the items in, and marked off, the checklist at the bottom of the exercise.